How English Became English

How English Became English

A Short History of a Global Language

SIMON HOROBIN

OXFORD
UNIVERSITY PRESS

OXFORD

UNIVERSITY PRESS

Great Clarendon Street, Oxford, OX2 6DP,
United Kingdom

Oxford University Press is a department of the University of Oxford.
It furthers the University's objective of excellence in research, scholarship,
and education by publishing worldwide. Oxford is a registered trade mark of
Oxford University Press in the UK and in certain other countries

Published in the United States of America by Oxford University Press
198 Madison Avenue, New York, NY 10016, United States of America

British Library Cataloguing in Publication Data

Data available

Library of Congress Control Number: 2015952191

ISBN 978–0–19–875427–5

Printed in Great Britain by
Clays Ltd, St Ives plc

For Jennifer, Lucy, Rachel, and Florence

For Jessica, Lucy, Rachel, and Florence

CONTENTS

Acknowledgements   ix
List of Illustrations   xi

1. What is English?   1
2. Origins   14
3. Authorities   39
4. Standards   72
5. Varieties   99
6. Global Englishes   131
7. Why Do We Care?   152

Further Reading   167
Index   171

ACKNOWLEDGEMENTS

I am very grateful to Andrea Keegan who commissioned this book and to anonymous reviewers for their incisive comments on previous drafts. I also wish to thank Jenny Nugee, who provided much helpful guidance throughout the writing process. I am grateful to the President and Fellows of Magdalen College, Oxford, for permission to reproduce MS lat. 105, and to Christine Ferdinand and James Fishwick for their assistance. This book has benefited from the insights and advice of numerous friends and colleagues; in particular I wish to thank Deborah Cameron, who read the entire book in draft and made many helpful suggestions, Lynda Mugglestone, Charlotte Brewer, Jeremy Smith, David Crystal, Tim Machan, and Seth Lerer. I am also grateful to my students, especially Lucy Diver, Rosie Durkin, John Phipps, Molly Janz, Alice Richardson, Luc Rosenberg, Jack Solloway, Alice Theobald, and Alice Troy-Donovan, for many fruitful discussions of the issues raised here while I was writing this book. I alone remain responsible for the opinions and for any inaccuracies that remain.

LIST OF ILLUSTRATIONS

1 The future of English? CartoonStock.com.   12

2 The Indo-European language family tree.   16

3 A manuscript of Bede's *Historia Ecclesiastica
Gentis Anglorum*. Magdalen College, Oxford,
MS lat. 105, f. 99r. The President and
Fellows of Magdalen College, Oxford.   22

4 The language of medicine. CartoonStock.com.   34

5 The greengrocer's apostrophe. Duncan Cumming.   37

6 The problem of literally. *The New Yorker*,
Condé Nast.   44

7 The ultimate authority? H. W. Fowler,
A Dictionary of Modern English Usage (1926), title page.
Public Domain.   51

8 List of top sources cited in the *Oxford English
Dictionary*, 3rd edition. OED.com.   59

9 Dialect map: words used to refer to a cow-shed in
England and Wales. a NATCECT publication, courtesy
of the University of Sheffield.   115

10 Calvin and Hobbes on 'verbing'. Calvin and
Hobbes © 1993 Watterson. Reprinted with
permission of Universal Uclick. All rights reserved.   125

List of Illustrations

11 Kachru's model of global Englishes. Public Domain.   139

12 Advertisement in Singlish. Pulai Ubin,
    Singapore. Michael Elleray/Wikimedia.   143

13 Fewer or less? *The New Yorker*, Condé Nast.   157

What is English?

ENGLISH. *adj.*
Belonging to England; thence English is the language
of England.

Samuel Johnson, *Dictionary of the English Language* (1755)

Samuel Johnson's straightforward identification of English
as the language of England hardly begins to capture the
diversity and complexity of the language's use in the twenty-
first century; English today is spoken by approximately
450 million people all over the world. But the language
used by its many speakers varies, in pronunciation, spelling,
grammar, and vocabulary, to such an extent that it seems
necessary to ask whether these people can all be considered
to be speaking English. Even more people speak English as
a second language, with figures varying from 1 billion to
1.5 billion people, and with considerably greater levels of
linguistic divergence. Are all these people speaking the same
language, or are we witnessing the emergence of new Englishes? Since more than half of the world's native English
speakers live in the USA, we might wonder whether the
balance of power has shifted such that to speak 'English'

today is to speak General American rather than Standard British English. Does English no longer 'belong to England', as Dr Johnson confidently claimed, but rather to the USA, or to everyone who wishes to employ it?

English has been in use for 1,500 years; during that time it has changed to such an extent that the form of the language used by the Anglo-Saxons is unrecognizable to contemporary English speakers. Today we refer to this language as Old English, but should we perhaps think of it as a different language altogether? Modern Italian is descended from the Latin spoken by the Romans, but these are considered to be different languages. Might that not also be true of Old English and Modern English?

The following sections contain five different translations of the same passage from the New Testament (Luke 15: 11–16). Despite being very different, each of these has a claim to represent a kind of English. But are they all forms of English, or different languages in their own right? What criteria should we apply when attempting to make such distinctions?

Old English

He cwæð: soðlice sum man hæfde twegen suna. þa cwæð se yldra to his fæder; Fæder. syle me minne dæl minre æhte þe me to gebyreð: þa dælde he him his æhte; þa æfter feawa dagum ealle his þing gegaderude se gingra sunu: and ferde wræclice on feorlen rice. and forspilde þar his æhta lybbende on his gælsan; þa he hig hæfde ealle amyrrede þa wearð mycel hunger on þam rice and he wearð wædla; þa

ferde he and folgude anum burhsittendan men þæs rices ða
sende he hine to his tune þæt he heolde his swyn; þa
gewilnode he his wambe gefyllan of þam biencoddun þe
ða swyn æton. and him man ne sealde.

Given how different the language of this extract is from Modern English, you may be wondering how it could be considered a form of English at all. It is taken from a translation into Old English—the scholarly term that refers to the language used by the Germanic tribes who invaded and settled in Britain in the fifth century AD up to the Norman Conquest in 1066. But, while its vocabulary may appear quite unrelated to that of Modern English, this is in part the consequence of a different spelling system—including the letters 'þ' 'thorn', 'æ' 'ash', and 'ð' 'eth', which are no longer used in English. If we look closely, we can spot a number of familiar words, such as *sunu*, *fæder*, and *tune*, which are the ancestors of Modern English *son*, *father*, and *town*. Other words are harder to recognize, but are neverthe-less demonstrably the root of the Modern English equiva-lent: *mycel* 'much', *twegen* 'two', *dæl* 'dole'. All of these are English words, yet their spellings and pronunciations have changed so that we no longer immediately recognize them as such.

In other cases, it is not just the spelling and pronunciation that have changed. The word *sylle* is the origin of our Modern English word *sell*, but here it means 'give'; similarly, *wambe* is Modern English *womb*, but here it refers to the stomach. If we turn from the lexical, or content, words in the passage to its grammatical items—prepositions, pronouns, and conjunctions—we find that many are identical to

3

their Modern English equivalents: *he, him, his, me, and, to*. But, despite these clear correspondences, this Old English extract remains significantly different from Modern English, to the extent that contemporary speakers of English are unable to read it without special study.

Early Modern English

> And hee said, A certaine man had two sonnes: And the yonger of them said to his father, Father, giue me the portion of goods that falleth to me. And he diuided vnto them his liuing. And not many dayes after, the yonger sonne gathered al together, and tooke his iourney into a farre countrey, and there wasted his substance with riotous liuing. And when he had spent all, there arose a mighty famine in that land, and he beganne to be in want. And he went and ioyned himselfe to a citizen of that countrey, and he sent him into his fields to feed swine. And he would faine haue filled his belly with the huskes that the swine did eate: & no man gaue vnto him.

This second example, taken from the Authorized, or King James, Version of the Bible published in 1611, is much closer to Modern English. Considering it was written four hundred years ago, it is striking how easy it is for a contemporary English speaker to understand. Although some of the vocabulary sounds old-fashioned, most of the words are still in use, albeit not always with the same meaning. Words like *liuing*, *substance*, *swine*, *fain*, and *vnto* lend the passage an archaic and formal feel, but present few barriers to comprehension. By contrast, the use of the word *belly* strikes a discordant note, since it seems oddly colloquial for such a serious context.

The seemingly random sprinkling of 'e's at the ends of words contributes to the olde Englishe appearance; other spelling differences include the interchangeable use of 'u' and 'v'—compare *gaue* and *vnto*—and 'i' where Modern English employs 'j', *iourney*—the Modern English distribution of i/j and u/v was not established until the eighteenth century. Grammatical distinctions are minor; instead of *did eat*, Modern English would now say *ate*. The syntax of the passage varies from Modern English translations in preferring a paratactic sentence structure—one that begins each new sentence with the conjunction *and*—a device that is condemned by modern style guides as clumsy and childish.

Scots

> This, tae, he said tae them: 'There wis aince a man hed twa sons; an ae day the yung son said til him, "Faither, gie me the faa-share o your haudin at I hae a richt til". Sae the faither haufed his haudin atweesh his twa sons. No lang efterhin the yung son niffert the haill o his portion for siller, an fuir awa furth til a faur-aff kintra, whaur he sperfelt his siller livin the life o a weirdless waister. Efter he hed gane throu the haill o it, a fell faimin brak out i yon laund, an he faund himsel in unco mister. Sae he gaed an hired wi an indwaller i that kintra, an the man gied him the wark o tentin his swine outbye i the fields. Gledlie wad he panged his wame wi the huils at they maitit the swine wi, but naebodie gied him a haet'.

This third version is much less clearly recognizable as a form of English; it is in fact a translation into Modern Scots by William Laughton Lorimer, published in 1983. But, as with the Old English translation, many of the most basic words—grammatical items and common nouns—are identical to those of Modern English: *this*, *he*, *said*, *them*, *there*, *man*, *your*, *and*, *the*, and so on. Other words are evidently related to Modern English equivalents, once we make allowance for the different spelling: *richt* 'right', *faither* 'father', *gie* 'give', *twa* 'two', *aince* 'once', *lang* 'long'. Some of these reflect different spelling conventions, while others point to alternative pronunciations.

But this is not simply English with an accent, since not all differences can be explained as the result of spelling and pronunciation changes. Some of the words have no recognizable English equivalent. This is the result of Scots borrowing words from other languages, such as *niffert* 'exchanged', from Old Norse, *sperfelt* 'scattered', from Old French, and *panged* 'stuffed', from Middle Dutch. The word *fell* 'cruel' (related to the word *felon*) does survive into Modern English, but only in the phrase *one fell swoop*—often mistakenly confused with *foul*.

As well as these lexical differences there are grammatical distinctions, such as the use of the demonstrative pronoun *yon*, not found in Standard English. Even the innocuous preposition *til* 'to', a borrowing from Old Norse, attests to a different history for this variety; although *til* is not used in Standard English, it is still found in northern dialects of English, testifying to the close historical relationship between Scots and northern English. While Scots and

English evidently have much in common, Scots is more intimately connected to the northern English dialects rather than its standard form. Other differences set Scots apart from English entirely, testifying to its long history as an independent language.

Tok Pisin

> *Na Jisas i tok moa olsem, 'Wanpela man i gat tupela pikinini man. Na namba 2 pikinini i tokim papa olsem, "Papa, mi ting long olgeta samting yu laik tilim long mi wantaim brata bilong mi. Hap bilong mi, mi laik bai yu givim long mi nau". Orait papa i tilim olgeta samting bilong en i go long tupela. I no longtaim, na dispela namba 2 pikinini i bungim olgeta samting bilong en na i salim long ol man. Na em i kisim mani na i go i stap long wanpela longwe ples. Em i stap long dispela ples, na em i mekim ol kain kain hambak pasin, na olgeta mani bilong en i pinis. Na taim olgeta mani bilong en i pinis, taim bilong bikpela hangre i kamap long dispela ples. Na em i no gat wanpela samting. Olsem na em i go kisim wok long wanpela man bilong dispela ples. Na dispela man i salim em i go long banis pik bilong en bilong lukautim ol pik. Em i lukim ol pik i kaikai ol skin bilong bin, na em i gat bikpela laik tru long kisim sampela na pulapim bel bilong en. Tasol i no gat wanpela man i givim kaikai long em'.*

This fourth extract is undoubtedly the hardest to justify as an example of English, since it appears to bear few similarities to the language spoken today. The translation is in Tok Pisin, one of three official languages spoken in Papua

New Guinea. But, while the language of this extract may appear entirely foreign, some of the grammatical and core lexical items are those of Modern English: *man, yu, mi, bilong, gat, samting*, albeit with differences in spelling indicative of alternative pronunciations. There are other words that, although their English origin is no longer evident, are derived from Modern English equivalents; the word *pela*, for instance, originates in the English word *fellow*. But, while such connections point to a shared heritage, the role of the word *pela* sets Tok Pisin apart from English. In Tok Pisin, *pela* functions as a grammatical ending added to nouns to mark when they are plural, demonstrating a major difference in the grammatical structures of Tok Pisin and English.

The reason for the connections we have observed is that Tok Pisin is an English-language creole—a term used to refer to a simplified version of English mixed with one or more other languages, employed by non-native speakers as a lingua franca (a language used as a means of communication by speakers of different languages). Are English language creoles like Tok Pisin additional forms of English, or languages in their own right? Given their reduced vocabulary and simplified grammar, is it appropriate to think of creoles, and the more basic form known as a pidgin, as languages at all? Are they better considered as evidence of idiosyncratic and failed attempts to acquire English, similar to the crude efforts found in the spam emails offering highly lucrative business proposals that flood our inboxes?

Modern English

> *Jesus continued: 'There was a man who had two sons. The younger one said to his father, "Father, give me my share of the estate". So he divided his property between them. Not long after that, the younger son got together all he had, set off for a distant country and there squandered his wealth in wild living. After he had spent everything, there was a severe famine in that whole country, and he began to be in need. So he went and hired himself out to a citizen of that country, who sent him to his fields to feed pigs. He longed to fill his stomach with the pods that the pigs were eating, but no one gave him anything'.*

This final example may seem uncontroversial, since it is self-evidently a translation into standard Modern English. But, while we call this English, many of the key terms it employs, *estate*, *property*, *divided*, *spent*, *famine*, *country*, *citizen*, and *stomach*, are borrowings from other languages. Since English includes numerous loanwords of this kind, many of which have been in use for centuries, this reliance upon foreign words may appear entirely unobjectionable. Yet the extent to which the English language should rely on words borrowed from foreign sources, rather than preferring ones of Old English origin, has been hotly debated for centuries, and continues to be contested today by proponents of pure English.

Attempts to create a purer form of English can be traced back to the sixteenth century. Sir John Cheke (1514–1557), noted linguist and Professor of Greek at Cambridge University, was so determined that the English tongue should be preserved 'pure, unmixt and unmangeled with borowing of other tunges' that he produced a translation of the gospel of St Matthew using only native words, forcing him to coin neologisms ('new words') such as *mooned* 'lunatic', *hundreder* 'centurion', and *crossed* 'crucified'. This policy recalls an Old English practice in which Latin words like *discipulus* were rendered using native formations like *leorningcniht*, or 'learning-follower', rather than by borrowing the Latin word, as Modern English does with *disciple*.

Attempts to fashion a purer form of literary English can be seen in the poetry of Edmund Spenser in the sixteenth century and William Barnes in the nineteenth century. Barnes' arguments against borrowing were primarily directed at perspicuity and ease of understanding—although his proposed replacements, such as *two-horned rede-ship* 'dilemma', *one-head thing-name* 'proper noun', and *fore-begged thought-putting* 'hypothetical proposition', were arguably no less opaque. Yet the debate about linguistic purity cannot be divorced from one of nationalism; for Barnes, borrowing, or what he dismissively referred to as 'Gallicizing, Latinizing, and Hellenizing', was a 'proof of national inferiority'—an admission that English was insufficient for its purposes and must rely on other languages to make good its weaknesses.

The concern with clarity was taken up by George Orwell in his 1945 essay, 'Politics and the English Language'. Orwell lamented the way bad writers are 'haunted by the notion that Latin or Greek words are grander than Saxon ones'. Today's plain English movements continue to campaign for the use of straightforward words in place of pompous jargon—frequently a case of preferring a native word over a foreign borrowing.

What is the status of foreign words in English today? Should we be restricting the number of words adopted from other languages? Are foreign words corrupting the purity of the English tongue, leaving it impoverished and capable only of unintelligible gobbledygook, or do borrowed words add to the diversity and richness of English?

I might have added a further version to the translations of the Bible quoted in the previous sections: one rendered into text speech by the Bible Society of Australia. Commissioned in 2005 in order to make the Bible more accessible to young people and to harness new technology to facilitate distribution, this version employs the abbreviations typical of SMS texting. It opens: 'In da Bginnin God cre8d da heavens & da earth.' Does the prevalence of this kind of writing herald the emergence of a new kind of English, or are such creative reworkings merely a passing fad? Is this an acceptable form of communication, or a corruption of correct English spelling and grammar? By giving text speech legitimacy in this way, are we accepting lower standards of literacy, and thereby condemning future generations to a lifetime of underachievement? Or is this how we will all be writing English in the future, as digital media become increasingly central to learning and communication? (See Figure 1).

Each of these translations raises different questions about the status of the English language, its linguistic forebears, and progeny. To answer these questions, the following chapters will look back at where English came from, and how it has developed into the language used throughout the world today. As the balance of power shifts from the traditional authorities—dictionaries, style guides, and the

Figure 1 The future of English?

British upper classes—we will consider what the future holds for Standard British English. Will it retain its status as a prestige variety of English, recognized and valued throughout the world, or will other regional standards challenge its position? Will the future see more pidginization, as compromise varieties like Euro English emerge, forged in the boardrooms of international business and the corridors of the European parliament? As American English increases its dominance, will it come to replace British English, or will the two languages develop independently, so that George Bernard Shaw's quip about England and the USA being 'separated by a common language' will become truer than he imagined?

2
Origins

Where does the English language come from? Since there are many correspondences between Modern English and Modern French—think of common words like *money*, *fruit*, *chamber*, *table*—it is often thought that the two languages are closely related. Since French is a Romance language, one derived from Latin, it is presumed that English is from the same source. This assumption gains support from the large number of English words of Latin origin; common words like *village*, *picture*, and *figure* all descend from Latin. But these correspondences relate to individual words rather than grammatical structure, and consequently are of less significance when tracing the origins of a language.

While it is true that a language inherits much of its vocabulary from earlier stages in its history, it is also common for words to be borrowed from other, unrelated, languages. Modern English includes words from a variety of different languages, such as *tea* (Chinese), *curry* (Tamil), *sugar* (Arabic), but these words are the result of later contact through trade rather than genetic inheritance. Such words may give the appearance of a genetic affiliation, but, to determine whether such correspondences are indicative of a genuine relationship, we must turn to the earliest forms of the language.

Beginnings

The earliest recorded form of English is known as Old English—a language used by the Anglo-Saxons, as well as other Germanic tribes, who came to Britain from continental Europe in the fifth century, following the withdrawal of the Roman legions. Despite the disparate origins of the various Germanic tribes who settled in the British Isles during this period, they eventually came to consider themselves a single people and adopted the name of the Angles, from which the word *English* is derived.

The Germanic dialects spoken by these tribes descend from a single, common ancestor, known to linguists as 'Proto-Germanic', which dates back to around 200 BC. Since the speakers of Proto-Germanic were illiterate and so left no written records, we have to rely entirely on a process of 'hypothetical reconstruction'—the establishment of a plausible form based on comparison of attested forms in related languages—to gain insights into the language at this stage in its history. Proto-Germanic is itself part of a larger language family known as Indo-European, which is the origin of most modern European languages, as well as some used today in Asia. The relationships between these various language groups may be schematized using the family-tree model shown in Figure 2—a model also employed by genealogists and evolutionary biologists.

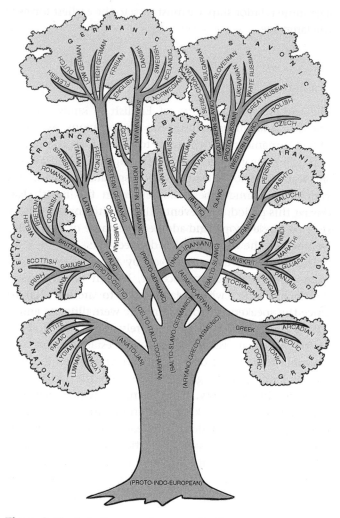

Figure 2 The Indo-European language family tree.

Comparison of the earliest recorded states of these languages reveals a common core of words that, despite differences in spelling and pronunciation, reflect a single shared ancestor. Equivalents of the Modern English kinship terms *mother*, *brother*, and *sister* are recorded in most Indo-European languages, and take us back to the remotest stages of that language.

Although a member of the Indo-European language family, the Germanic group underwent a series of changes to its consonants that set it apart from the other constituent languages. Because the first systematic description of this change was the work of the German folklorist Jacob Grimm, it is known as Grimm's Law. This shift explains why Germanic languages have 'f' where other Indo-European languages have 'p'. Compare English *father*, German *Vater* (where 'v' is pronounced 'f'), Norwegian *far*, with Latin *pater*, French *père*, Italian *padre*, Sanskrit *pita*. Following its split from the Indo-European family, the Germanic group divided into three branches: West Germanic (English, German, Dutch, and Frisian), East Germanic (Gothic—the language of the Goths, spoken in the fourth century AD in the Black Sea area, but no longer in use), and North Germanic (Norwegian, Danish, Swedish, Icelandic).

Returning to our opening question about the origins of English, we can now see that, while English is distantly related to both Latin and French, it is principally a Germanic language; its closest modern linguistic relations are Dutch, German, and Frisian. This becomes especially clear when we examine the earliest Old English written records, which contain very few words of Latin origin and almost none from French. The Old English vocabulary, or 'lexicon', consists of words created using methods of word formation that are characteristic of Germanic languages: compound words, formed by joining two existing words, such as *dægesege*, literally 'day's eye', Modern English *daisy*, *haligdæg*, 'holy day', Modern English *holiday*, and words formed by affixation—the addition of prefixes and suffixes. The Old English word *unbrad*, 'narrow', was formed by adding the negative prefix 'un-' to the adjective *brad*, 'broad'—literally 'unbroad'. Another common method of forming words in Old English was conversion: transferring a word from one word class to another; this can be seen in the formation of the verb *dagian*, 'to dawn', from the noun *dæg*, 'day'.

Although contact with other languages has radically altered the nature of its vocabulary, English today remains a Germanic language at its core. The words that describe family relationships—*father*, *mother*, *brother*, *son*—are of Old English descent (compare Modern German *Vater*, *Mutter*, *Bruder*, *Sohn*), as are the terms for body parts, such as *foot*, *finger*, *shoulder* (German *Fuß*, *Finger*, *Schulter*), and numerals, *one*, *two*, *three*, *four*, *five* (German *eins*, *twei*, *drei*, *vier*, *fünf*), as well as its grammatical words, such as *and*, *for*, *I* (German *und*, *für*, *Ich*).

The sources of its lexicon are not the only clue to the English language's heritage; its Germanic origins are also apparent from its grammatical structure, such as the formation of the preterite, or past, tense. Modern English has two methods of forming the preterite: changing the stem vowel, as in *ride–rode* (known as 'strong' verbs), or adding a suffix, as in *walk–walked* ('weak' verbs). The strong verb is the older of the two classes; the practice of changing the stem vowel to form different parts of the verb can be traced back to proto-Indo-European. The weak verb class is a newer innovation, probably formed by adding a part of the verb *do* to the stem, and is found only in the Germanic languages; compare modern German *mach* 'do'–*machte* 'did'. Weak verbs are now the dominant class in Modern English, so that new coinages automatically form their past tense this way. The past tense of *to Google* is *Googled*; even a verb like *jive*, which would fit neatly into the *ride–rode* class, becomes *jived* rather than *jove*.

But, while this grammatical feature links English with the Germanic family, there are other aspects of Germanic languages that are missing from English. Perhaps most striking is the comparatively little use English makes of the endings, or 'inflexions', employed by other Germanic languages to carry grammatical information such as number, case, and gender. But while inflexional endings are limited to the possessive and plural '-s' endings in Modern English (*boys*, *boy's*), much greater use is made of them in Old English.

Like modern Germanic languages, Old English employed a system of inflexional endings that distinguished number (singular, plural, and the dual—used to refer to two and only two) and four cases: nominative (subject), accusative (direct object), genitive (possession), dative (indirect object). Old English also had a system whereby nouns were classified into three separate categories, known as genders: masculine, feminine, and neuter; this three-way grammatical gender system is still found in Modern German. The choice of category had nothing to do with sex, or real-world gender, so that the noun *wif*, 'woman', was neuter (just as German *Weib* 'woman' is also neuter), while *wifmann*, the origin of Modern English *woman*, was masculine. Old English also attests to a system of 'agreement'; where Modern English has just one definite article, *the*, Old English had alternative forms to enable the article to agree with its corresponding noun according to case, gender, and number.

By turning to its earliest recorded forms, we can see that the English language began life as a typical member of the Germanic language family. Since the Old English period, English has undergone a number of substantial changes, which have radically altered its structure, vocabulary, pronunciation, and spelling. The following brief history of the language will give an account of the most important of these changes.

Old English (AD 650–1100)

Although I have highlighted the Germanic origins of the English language, it is important to be aware of the multi-lingual nature of Britain from the Anglo-Saxon period to the present day. Contact with speakers of different languages has resulted in numerous changes to English—especially its vocabulary.

In his *Historia Ecclesiastica Gentis Anglorum* (AD 731) (*Ecclesiastical History of the English People*), the Anglo-Saxon historian Bede listed five languages used in Britain: English, British (Welsh), Irish, Pictish (spoken in northern Scotland), and Latin (see Box 1). Contact between speakers of Celtic languages and the Anglo-Saxons has left few traces in

---

BOX 1 *The earliest English poem*
··

Although Bede wrote in Latin, his *Historia* includes a remarkable account of the oldest surviving poem composed in the English language. The story recounts how an illiterate lay-brother at the monastery at Whitby, named Cædmon, was miraculously given the gift of poetry by an angel who appeared to him in a dream. Much of Cædmon's subsequent output has been lost, although a short poem in praise of creation survives, known as Cædmon's *Hymn*. Bede translated the poem into Latin, but later scribes added the work in its original form into the margins of manuscripts of the *Historia*. Figure 3 shows a leaf from a manuscript of Bede's *Historia* produced in England during the twelfth century. In the margin you can see where the Old English text of the *Hymn* has been added.

Translation into Modern English:

Now we must praise the guardian of the heavenly kingdom, the Ordainer's might and his conception, the work of the Father of glory: as he, the eternal Lord, established the beginning of every wonder; he, holy Creator, first created heaven as a roof for the children of men; he, mankind's guardian, eternal Lord, almighty Ruler, afterwards made for men the middle-earth, the world.

Modern English. This is because, following the Anglo-Saxon invasions, Celtic speakers took refuge in the extreme west and north of Britain—locations which have remained Celtic-speaking until the present day, or, in the case of Cornwall, until the eighteenth century. Where there was contact between Celtic speakers and Anglo-Saxons, the balance of power was firmly in the direction of the

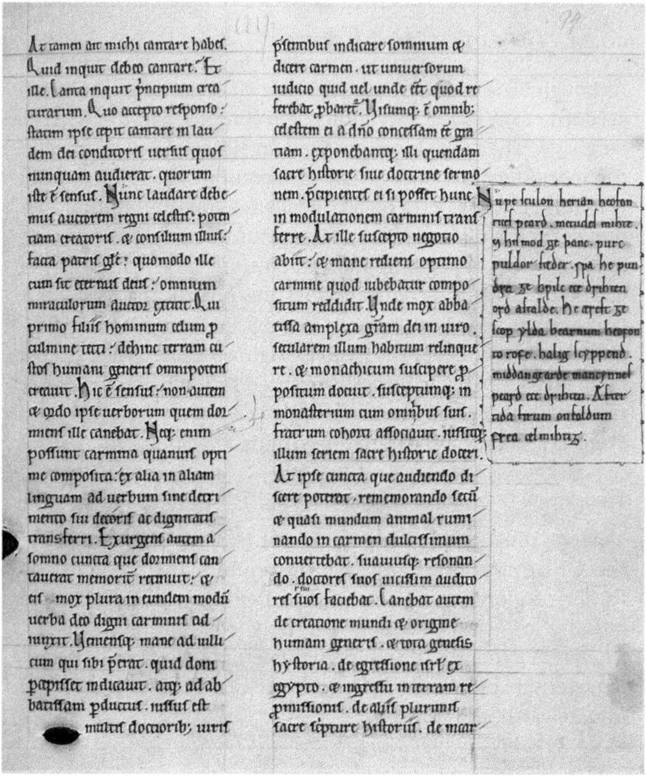

Figure 3 A manuscript of Bede's *Historia Ecclesiastica Gentis Anglorum*. Magdalen College, Oxford, MS lat. 105, f. 99r.

Anglo-Saxons, for whom the Celts served as slaves. This is evidenced by the use of the Old English word *wealh*, the ancestor of the place-name Wales and the second element of Cornwall, which could mean both Briton and slave. Because of this, Celtic influence is largely restricted to names of places and rivers, such as Avon, from the Celtic word for 'river', and Ouse, the Celtic word for 'water'. The county names Kent and Devon are both of Celtic origin, as is the first element of Cumberland, whose name translates as 'land of the Welsh'.

As we have seen, Old English drew upon its own resources to coin new terms, rather than borrowing words from other languages. The prominence of Latin, especially in its role as the language of Christianity, brought to Britain in AD 597 by missionaries sent from Rome by Pope Gregory the Great, did, however, trigger the adoption of a number of words relating to the new faith. Most of these are specialized terms, unlikely to have figured much in the spoken language: *apostol*, 'apostle' (Latin *apostolus*); *abbod*, 'abbot' (Latin *abbas*); *scol*, 'school' (Latin *schola*); *magister*, 'master' (Latin *magister*). In some cases, technical terms borrowed from Latin replaced the native equivalent, as happened with the Old English compound *stæfcræft* 'letter-craft'—that is, 'grammar'—which was ousted by *grammaticcræft*.

Latin enjoyed a long lifespan in England, thanks particularly to its use as the language of scholarship and the Church, though it was never a first language, and was employed more in writing than in speech. Despite the predominantly scholarly and literary nature of the Latin loans adopted in Old English, some words entered the core vocabulary through direct contact with Roman soldiers, perhaps dating back to the period before the Anglo-Saxon invasions. Latin influence of this kind can be seen in the adoption of words like *win*, 'wine' (Latin *vinum*); *strœt*, 'street' (Latin *via strata* 'paved road'); and *ceaster*, 'city' (Latin *castra*), found in modern place names like *Winchester* and *Manchester*.

The Anglo-Saxons also came into contact with a North Germanic language known today as Old Norse, spoken by the Danes and Norwegians who ravaged, and eventually settled in, the north and east of England from the 870s up to the end of the eleventh century. Where Latin loanwords were largely restricted to the ecclesiastical, written medium, Old Norse penetrated English in a more radical way. While Latin was a spoken language, it remained an acquired second language rather than a native tongue, whose use was mostly confined to the cloister. Old Norse was primarily a spoken vernacular—one that would have been frequently employed in interactions between Vikings and Anglo-Saxons. Because the two languages were closely related (as members of the Germanic group), it is likely that they would have been mutually comprehensible, further encouraging the transfer of words from one language to the other.

Where Latin loanwords were predominantly lexical words—nouns, verbs, adjectives, adverbs—Old Norse loans included grammatical items such as pronouns, conjunctions, and prepositions. Where Latin borrowings were highly specialized words found exclusively in writing, Old Norse supplied everyday words commonly found in speech; these include *cast*, *egg*, *husband*, *ill*, *knife*, *leg*, *take*, *though*, *ugly, want, window*; even the kinship term *sister* is a Norse borrowing (Old English used the related *sweostor*). The most striking effect of this contact is the adoption into English of the Old Norse third-person plural pronouns, *they, their*, and *them*, which replaced the Old English equivalents to enable clearer distinctions between the third-person plural pronouns *hie* ('they'), *hira* ('their'), *him* ('them'), and the pronouns *he, her*, and *him*.

Owing to a major pronunciation difference between the North and West Germanic languages, Old Norse is the origin of many words that begin with a hard 'sk' sound in English today, such as *sky* and *skin*; in West Germanic languages like Old English, this sound became 'sh'. This explains the existence of pairs of words like *skirt* and *shirt*; these words derive from the same Germanic root, but the first comes via Old Norse and the second directly from Old English. Old Norse also left its mark on place names, particularly in the areas of densest Viking settlement (the East Midlands and the north). These include *by*, 'farm'; *thorp*, 'village'; *thwaite*, 'clearing, meadow'; *toft*, 'piece of ground'—found in the names of places such as *Enderby, Grimsthorpe, Bassenthwaite*, and *Sibbertoft*.

Another effect of contact between speakers of Old English and Old Norse was the simplification of the Old English system of grammatical inflexions: the endings added to words which carry grammatical information. While there was considerable overlap in the vocabulary of these two languages, Old Norse employed a distinct set of inflexional endings. In order to facilitate communication, the two groups of speakers must have placed less stress on the inflexional endings; as a consequence, the Old English system of inflexions began to break down.

By the end of the Old English period, Anglo-Saxon manuscripts show considerable blurring of these distinctions; by 1500 the majority of the endings had been lost entirely. The only traces of the system of noun inflexion that remain today are the 's' ending added to indicate possession (the genitive case)—*the boy's book*—and the 's' added to mark plurality—*the books* (alongside the much less common '-en' ending preserved in *oxen* and *children*).

The erosion of these inflexional endings also triggered the breakdown of the grammatical gender system, which relied upon this system. A further contributing factor was the tendency for speakers to default to real-world gender when making reference to animate objects; rather than referring to a woman as *it*, it became common for speakers to use the feminine pronoun *she*.

Another linguistic connection between the Anglo-Saxons who settled in the British Isles and other Germanic tribes is their use of the runic alphabet, developed on the continent for scratching short messages onto wood or stone. But runic writing had only a limited use in Britain; the conversion to Christianity brought with it the Roman alphabet, which was established as the principal medium for Old English written records. Because it was devised for writing Latin rather than English, the Roman alphabet was not a perfect fit for the Old English sound system. Latin had no 'th' sound and consequently no letter to represent it; to fill this gap the Anglo-Saxons imported the letter 'thorn', 'þ', from the runic alphabet. This letter remained in use for writing

English until the fifteenth century, when it developed a y-shaped appearance; it now survives in this modified form in faux archaic *ye olde tea shoppe* signs, where *ye* should properly be pronounced 'the'.

English spelling began life as a comparatively transparent way of encoding the spoken language using written symbols, but as it became more fixed it ceased to keep step with changes in pronunciation. Since Anglo-Saxon scribes established the conventions for writing Old English, the spelling of Old English tends to be more phonetic than that of Modern English. Where Modern English speakers have become accustomed to the frustrations presented by the silent letters in words like *knight*, *gnat*, and *write*, such spellings would have been entirely logical to an Anglo-Saxon for whom these words were pronounced with initial 'k', 'g', and 'w'. The spelling of vowels was similarly transparent, so that words spelled with a double 'oo' were pronounced with a long 'oo' sound in Old English. Subsequent changes mean that the spelling of such words is no longer a reliable guide to their pronunciation in Modern English—compare *good*, *food*, and *blood*.

Middle English (1100–1500)

The shift from Old English to Middle English is usually dated to 1100, since the Norman Conquest of 1066, and the subsequent impact of the French language, were major factors in triggering the changes that characterize this linguistic transition. The Normans were originally Scandinavians—the name Norman derives from the earlier Northman—but

27

had settled in northern France in the early tenth century. The French used in England immediately after the conquest, known to scholars as Anglo-Norman, was originally restricted to the aristocrats and noblemen who supported William of Normandy. Over the following two centuries this language was adopted by a wider social group, though by the fourteenth century it had ceased to be acquired as a native tongue and was largely restricted to administrative use.

During this period a large number of words were borrowed into English from French. Differences in their spelling and pronunciation from the equivalents in the Central French dialect (the ancestor of Standard French today) demonstrate that they were adopted from the Norman French dialect: the Modern English word *war* derives from Norman French *werre* rather than from standard French *guerre*. In some cases both the Norman French and Central French forms have been taken into English, as in the case of *warranty* and *guarantee*, where the former term has become restricted to legal usage. Unlike Old English and Old Norse, Anglo-Norman and Middle English were not mutually comprehensible. Where Norse speakers settled among the Anglo-Saxons, Anglo-Norman speakers occupied positions of power and authority. This is reflected in the patterns of lexical borrowing; the earliest French loans recorded in English are concerned with the establishment of Anglo-Norman government, and include words like *justice, chancellor, prison, noble, crime*, and *court*.

During the first two centuries following the conquest, English was largely restricted to speech, and most writing of this period was in one of the more authoritative languages—French or Latin. By the fourteenth century, the status of English had begun to change, as a result of major social upheavals following the Black Death, and the emergence of accomplished English language writers such as Geoffrey Chaucer (*c*.1343–1400).

French continued to occupy a prestigious place in English society, especially the Central French dialect spoken in Paris. This prompted an increase in the numbers of French words borrowed, especially those relating to French society and culture. As a consequence, English words concerned with scholarship, fashion, the arts, and food—such as *college*, *robe*, *verse*, *beef*—are often drawn from French (even if their ultimate origins lie in Latin). The higher status of French in this period continues to influence the associations of pairs of synonyms in Modern English, such as *begin–commence*, *look–regard*, *stench–odour*. In each of these pairs, the French borrowing is of a higher register than the word inherited from Old English.

But French did not simply add words of a higher status; in many cases the French word was responsible for ousting the English word entirely, as in the case of Old English *wlonc*, replaced by Modern English *pride*. Even some kinship terms, such as Old English *eam* and *sweostor–sunu* ('sister–son'), were ousted by the French equivalents *uncle* and *nephew*.

Latin words continued to be borrowed during the Middle English period, though these were mostly drawn from the specialized areas of religion, learning, and the law: *scripture*, *history*, *allegory*, *client*, *executor*. Because French is itself derived from Latin, it is not always possible to determine whether a word entered English directly from Latin or via

French. The verb *incline*, for instance, which was spelled both as *enclinen* and *inclinen* in Middle English, may represent French *encliner* or Latin *inclinare*, or both.

The Middle English period also witnessed major changes to the spelling system. Following the Norman Conquest, French scribes began to draw upon their own spelling conventions when writing English: the Old English practice of using 'cw' in words like *cwen* was changed to 'qu', giving Modern English *queen*. French further complicated English spelling because many borrowings were introduced with their spelling unchanged. The spelling of loanwords was less of a problem during the Anglo-Saxon period, when fewer words were borrowed, and when the tendency was to respell them according to Old English practices. Hence a Greek loanword like *phoenix* was spelled *fenix*, preserving the Old English use of 'f' rather than 'ph'. But in Middle English, adoptions from French retained their spellings, introducing new sets of correspondences, such as the use of 'c' to represent 's' in French loans like *centre*, or 'ch' for 'sh' in words like *chef*.

Early Modern English (1500–1750)

The Early Modern period witnessed the biggest impact of Latin upon English—a direct consequence of the rediscovery of classical learning associated with the European renaissance. During this period, Latin continued to flourish as the language of scholarship: it was the medium of instruction in grammar schools, and the language of composition for scientific literature; Isaac Newton's foundational work on gravity, *Philosophiae Naturalis Principia Mathematica* (1687), was written in Latin.

However, during this period the functions of English were further elaborated, so that English came to be employed for a wider range of purposes; Newton wrote his later work *Opticks*, published in 1704, in English. The expansion of English was further encouraged by the Protestant Reformation, which promoted the translation of the Scriptures into English as a means of enabling direct access to the word of God. This vernacularization of specialist areas of science and religion created a need for technical terminology in English, such as *radius*, *lens*, *calculus*, and *vacuum*. The prominence of Latin meant that many words that had been borrowed from French during the Middle English period were reintroduced directly from Latin. These include the verb *compute* (Latin *computare*), which had already appeared in English as *count* (French *conter*) in the fourteenth century.

The high status accorded to the classical tongues in the Early Modern period meant that Latin and Greek words were adopted with their spellings intact—so we find Greek 'phi' spelled with a 'ph' rather than an 'f' in *philosophy* and *physics*. A reverence for Latinate spellings prompted the respelling of a number of words previously borrowed into English directly from French, whose origins lay in Latin. A silent 'b' was added to *debt* and *doubt* to align them with the Latin *debitum* and *dubitare*; a silent 'c' was inserted into *scissors* (Latin *scissor*); 'l' was introduced into *salmon* (Latin *salmo*), and a silent 'p' into *receipt* (Latin *receptum*). In most cases these silent letters drove spelling and pronunciation further apart, though in some instances, like *perfect* and *adventure* (Middle English *parfait* and *aventure*), the inserted letter is now sounded.

The expansion of trade and travel during this period led to contact with speakers of other European languages, especially Italian, Spanish, and Dutch. This resulted in further borrowings, especially relating to traded commodities. Italian loans adopted during this period include *parmesan* and *artichoke*, as well as architectural terms like *balcony* and *cupola*, and words relating to the arts: *stanza* and *violin*. Spanish loans reflect trading related to colonization—*anchovy*, *apricot*, *banana*, *cocoa*, *potato*, *tobacco*—while Dutch words include *guilder* and *excise*. Travel beyond Europe resulted in the introduction of words of Persian and Arabic extraction, borrowed via Turkish—*sherbet*, *yogurt*, *turban*, *divan*—and Indian loans: *cot*, *pundit*, *bungalow*, *dungaree*, *pukka*, *shampoo*. Settlement in North America led to the introduction of words from native American languages: *moccasin*, *moose*, *wigwam*, *skunk*.

The Early Modern period witnessed the most decisive and far-reaching changes in the history of English pronunciation: a systematic reorganization of the long vowel system, known today as the Great Vowel Shift. This process began in the fifteenth century and was completed by 1700; it is the main reason why Chaucer's pronunciation would sound very different to us today, whereas it is possible to watch a Shakespeare play in a reconstructed Original Pronunciation with few barriers of comprehension.

The Great Vowel Shift was triggered by a change from 'uu' (as in Modern English *flew*) to 'ow' in words like *now* and *cow*, and 'ii' (the sound in Modern English *see*) to 'iy' in words like *fine* and *life*. These replacements set in motion a further set of shifts that saw words like *goose* and *food*, previously pronounced with a long 'oo' sound (as in *road*), being pronounced with a long 'uu' sound, as in southern English accents today. In a similar way, words like *green* and *been*, which in Middle English were pronounced with a long 'ay' sound (similar to Modern English *way*), began to be pronounced with the long 'ii' sound, still used today. Since no corresponding changes were made to the spelling system, a further implication of the Great Vowel Shift was the increased disruption of the relationship between spelling and pronunciation.

Late Modern English (1750–1900)

During this period, the extension of scientific writing in English continued, in disciplines such as biology, chemistry, physics, and medicine, resulting in the expansion of specialist vocabulary. This comprised words borrowed directly from Latin and Greek, as well as neologisms formed by combining classical elements to produce pseudo-classical coinages. Examples include *invertebrate* (Latin *in* 'not' + *vertebra* 'joint'), *chlorophyll* (Greek *chloros* 'pale green' + *phyllon* 'leaf'), and words that mix Latin and Greek elements, such as *haemoglobin* (Greek *haima* 'blood' + Latin *globulus* 'globule'). This is why a visit to the doctor today can be such a linguistic challenge, even for a native English speaker, for whom terms like *gynaecology* (Greek *gyne* 'woman'), *obstretrics* (Latin *obstetrix* 'midwife'), and *geriatrics* (Greek *geras* 'old age'), are entirely opaque (see Figure 4).

"After looking at all your test results and consulting many experts, it's my medical opinion that you have something I can't pronounce."

Figure 4 *The language of medicine.*

During the eighteenth century, a fondness for French culture and manners led to the introduction of numerous French words. Where many of the French words adopted during the Middle English period now have anglicized pronunciations (for example, *centre* and *table*), words introduced at this time have generally retained their French spelling and sound, as in *liaison*, *beau*, and *faux pas*. The prominence of French culture in the eighteenth century prompted the respelling of some existing English words to reflect French practices; *bisket* began to be written *biscuit*, and *blew* was changed to *blue*.

The consequence of extensive borrowing from French, Latin, and Greek throughout the history of English is the creation of groups of synonyms occupying different registers (contexts within which they may be used): *freedom* and *liberty*; *happiness* and *felicity*; *depth* and *profundity*. Insights into the relationships between such synonyms can be gleaned by comparing their uses in forming new words. The Old English word *bird* gives us a term of abuse, *birdbrain*, Latin *avis* is the source of more technical words such as *aviation* and *aviary*, while Greek *ornith* is the root of exclusively scientific formations, such as *ornithology*.

Following the completion of the Great Vowel Shift, another change affected the long vowel system, bringing it closer to the system spoken today. Up until 1700 there was a distinction in pronunciation between words spelled with 'ea', like *meat*, and words written with 'ee' like *meet* (as is implied by the different spellings). During the eighteenth century these two groups of words merged, producing the Modern English situation where *sea* and *see* are pronounced identically. This merger led to a further confusion of the sound–spelling relationship in Modern English, since it meant that words with different spellings, like *meet/meat*, *sea/see*, were pronounced identically. There remain a handful of words which did not undergo this change; *break*, *great*, *steak*, *yea*, all preserve the earlier pronunciation.

During this period, the standardization of English spelling was largely completed; texts printed during the eighteenth and nineteenth centuries show few orthographic variations from Modern English. Differences in punctuation are few, although modern readers of eighteenth-century texts are often struck by the apparently random use made of capitalization. Far from being random, the custom developed of using capital letters as a means of making a word more prominent, or to emphasize its generality of reference, as in words like Truth, Beauty, and Ambition. Because printers, faced with the task of converting an author's handwritten manuscript into type, struggled to determine when a word was intended to be capitalized or not, they adopted the expediency of capitalizing all nouns. Since this practice had the effect of removing the potential for capitals to convey subtle nuances of meaning, authors responded by abandoning the practice so that by the nineteenth century our modern practice had been established.

One further difference from modern punctuation habits was the tendency to use the apostrophe when adding the plural 's' ending to foreign borrowings, such as *folio's* and *opera's*. This usage, known as the 'greengrocer's apostrophe' because it is thought to be particularly common in shops advertising *pear's*, *orange's*, and *apple's*, is highly stigmatized today (see Figure 5).

This brief overview of the history of English has shown that, while the family-tree model is a useful way of schematizing the language's origins, it cannot account fully for the relationship between English and other languages. This is because English has been affected at all linguistic levels—

Figure 5 The greengrocer's apostrophe.

pronunciation, spelling, grammar, and vocabulary—by the rich variety of tongues with which its users have come into contact.

We began by categorizing English as a member of the Germanic language family; but while this is historically accurate, it fails to capture the diverse relationships apparent in Modern English. By contrast, a language such as Modern German, with its continued employment of inflexional endings to indicate number, case, and gender, preserves its Germanic structure much more faithfully. Like Old English, Modern German still favours internal methods of word formation—affixation and compounding—over borrowing from other languages. Compare the English word *television*, a compound of two classical elements (Greek *telos* 'far' + Latin *visio* 'see'), with the German *Fernseher*, formed from the equivalent German words *fern* 'far' and *seher* 'seer'.

This overview has also revealed how English has been subject to far-reaching changes to its structure and vocabulary throughout its history. These are the result of contact with speakers of other languages, major social upheavals—invasion, conquest, plague—and the language's changing role in society. Like any living vernacular (a native language, not acquired artificially), the fortunes of the English language have been closely bound up with those of its speakers.

This should not surprise us; a language is a communicative tool manipulated by speakers within social networks. As these speakers, their communities, and societies vary, so the language and its functions are changed. Yet, despite this fact, many people view such alterations as evidence of corruption and decay, appealing to some form of Edenic perfection, from which the English language has fallen, owing to the misuse and neglect of its speakers. Like the Biblical account of Babel, in which an attempt to build a tower reaching to heaven results in God confounding their single language so that its speakers can no longer understand each other, speakers of English are considered to be corrupting their language in a way that is destined to result in total incomprehension.

But if a language is in the hands, or mouths, of its speakers, then who is to say that a particular usage is acceptable while another is not? Where does the authority lie for making such judgements? Or should that be *judgments*? These are questions we will address in Chapter 3.

3

Authorities

In this chapter we will consider how the rules of usage are established—where does the authority lie when questions of correctness are debated? Where do we turn to find answers to vexed questions of usage, such as whether it should be 'garidge' or 'garaadge', *disinterested* or *uninterested*, *minuscule* or *miniscule*, and in many other familiar debates? On what grounds can we state that Sarah Palin's neologism *refudiate* and George W. Bush's *misunderestimate* are not genuine words, but that Lisa Simpson's *meh* is?

The most obvious place to turn is to a dictionary, frequently held to be the ultimate authority in discussions of usage. But this is not as straightforward as it may seem. Where many people refer to 'the dictionary' as if there were a single such publication, the reality is considerably more complex. *Collins English Dictionary* (2014) includes an entry for the word *adorkable*, defined as 'socially inept or unfashionable in a charming or endearing way'; yet this word does not appear in the *Oxford English Dictionary*. Does this mean it is a legitimate word or not? Consulting a dictionary for an authoritative pronouncement is not as straightforward a solution as might initially appear.

Dictionaries

The view that a dictionary should set standards to be followed can be traced back to Dr Johnson's *Dictionary of the English Language* (1755). In the plan written before he had begun work on the project in 1747, addressed to his patron Lord Chesterfield, Johnson set out his conception of the work's function: 'This, my Lord, is my idea of an English dictionary, a dictionary by which the pronunciation of our language may be fixed, and its attainment facilitated; by which its purity may be preserved, its use ascertained [fixed], and its duration lengthened.'

Johnson based his dictionary upon examples extracted from writers before the Restoration, whose works he considered 'the wells of English undefiled'. By focusing on earlier English sources, Johnson sought to 'recall' the English language to its original 'Teutonick [Germanic] character' and away from the 'Gallick [French] structure' towards which it had been heading. Yet in the preface to the *Dictionary* itself, written with the benefit of years of lexicographical experience, Johnson recognized the futility of his hopes that his work would preserve the language from further change (see Box 2).

Although Johnson's *Dictionary* is often celebrated as the first such work in English, earlier instances of the monolingual dictionary can be traced in lists of hard words. The oldest example is Robert Cawdrey's *Table Alphabeticall* (1604), whose full title establishes its remit: *A Table Alphabeticall, conteyning and teaching the true writing, and vnderstanding of hard vsuall English wordes, borrowed*

BOX 2 *From the Preface to Johnson's* Dictionary of the English Language *(1755)*

BOX 2 *From the Preface to Johnson's* Dictionary of the English Language *(1755)*

....

'Those who have been persuaded to think well of my design, require that it should fix our language, and put a stop to those alterations which time and chance have hitherto been suffered to make in it without opposition. With this consequence I will confess that I flattered myself for a while; but now begin to fear that I have indulged expectation which neither reason nor experience can justify. When we see men grow old and die at a certain time one after another, from century to century, we laugh at the elixir that promises to prolong life to a thousand years; and with equal justice may the lexicographer be derided, who being able to produce no example of a nation that has preserved their words and phrases from mutability, shall imagine that his dictionary can embalm his language, and secure it from corruption and decay, that it is in his power to change sublunary nature, or clear the world at once from folly, vanity, and affectation.'

---

from the Hebrew, Greeke, Latine, or French. &c. This is a long way from the modern desk dictionary which aims to cover the most common English words, leaving more technical terminology to specialized lexicons. Far from being designed to assist with the correct use of words in regular use, Cawdrey's list began a tradition of glossing those terms borrowed from foreign languages: words like *concinnate*, *deambulate*, *pactation*, *refractarie*, whose meanings would have been particularly opaque to those who had not been educated in Latin and Greek—an audience Cawdrey himself characterizes as 'Ladies, Gentlewomen, or any other vnskilfull persons'.

In announcing his intention to supply the 'true writing, and vnderstanding' of the words he included, Cawdrey established the dictionary as a repository of linguistic authority for readers in search of certainty. Yet contemporary lexicographers reject such an approach, preferring instead to offer a descriptive account of current usage. As a result, modern dictionaries are continually revised to reflect new developments in spelling, pronunciation, and usage. This is what Steven Pinker, in his essay prefacing the *American Heritage Dictionary*, calls lexicography's (the craft of dictionary-making) 'dirty little secret': 'There's no one in charge; the lunatics are running the asylum.'

Today, the inclusion of slang words, acronyms, and terms deriving from social media, such as *amazeballs*, *YOLO*, and *selfie*, into updated editions of dictionaries often provoke consternation among the media and the general public, who see such words as unworthy of inclusion in such an authoritative repository. But, since these words are in widespread use among English speakers, it is proper that they should feature in a dictionary.

A longer lifespan is required for a word to find a place in the venerable *Oxford English Dictionary*; nevertheless, new inclusions and revisions to this work can provoke distress among its users. An adjustment to the entry for the adverb *literally* to include the sense 'figuratively', reflecting its widespread use as an intensifier—'I was literally gutted'—provides a classic example. According to a headline in *The Telegraph* newspaper in 2013, 'pedants will be in uproar after it was confirmed that the *Oxford English Dictionary* had included the erroneous use of the word "literally"'.

Typical of such reports is a conviction that a particular usage is incorrect, and that it should be the job of the lexicographers to rule against it. By appearing to endorse this supposed misuse, the *Oxford English Dictionary*'s editors are considered to be caving in to the low standards of sports pundits and teenagers, with whom this usage is traditionally associated. But, since the revision being reported had in fact been implemented two years before the story made the headlines, it appears not to have triggered the outrage predicted by *The Telegraph*.

Also missing from *The Telegraph*'s account is the fact that this use is accompanied by the label 'colloquial', and the following rider: 'Now one of the most common uses, although often considered irregular in standard English since it reverses the original sense of *literally* ("not figuratively or metaphorically")' (see Figure 6).

The popular view that a dictionary should uphold standards and prescribe, rather than reflect, usage was perhaps most strongly demonstrated by the furore that surrounded the publication of Webster's *Third New International Dictionary* in 1961, in which labels which had traditionally commented on the acceptability or otherwise of certain words were recast in a more neutral tone, reporting rather than dictating usage.

This change in policy provoked considerable hostility in the American press. *The New Yorker* printed a cartoon in which the receptionist at the Merriam-Webster company informed a visitor seeking an appointment with the

"Confound it, Hawkins, when I said I meant that literally, that was just a figure of speech."

Figure 6 The problem of literally.

dictionary's editor Philip Gove: 'Sorry, Dr. Gove ain't in'. This cartoon refers to the dictionary's apparent endorsement of the word *ain't*, which launched a volley of shocked newspaper headlines: 'You may have been taught it is uncouth to say "ain't." But it ain't.' The media's representation of the dictionary's treatment of *ain't* prompted the editor to release a statement intended to clarify his position. He noted that the word had been in use since the seventeenth century, and had appeared in Webster's dictionaries since 1890. He also drew attention to the accompanying usage note which highlighted its dubious status: 'disapproved by many and more common in less educated speech, used orally in most parts of the USA by many cultivated speakers.'

Webster's *Third* was based upon extensive analysis of usage, backed up by millions of citations; but, since Americans were used to a more openly prescriptive approach (a previous edition of Webster's had branded *ain't* 'illiterate'), many were dismayed by the tolerance being shown to usages they considered to be flatly wrong.

But while we might be tempted to dismiss such responses as driven by a misunderstanding of the function of a dictionary by those unwilling to confront the facts of usage, this would to be too simplistic. The dictionary's treatment of *ain't*—which included comments explicitly alerting its readers to the word's non-standard status—was evidently not sufficiently dogmatic for its shocked readers, who were especially distressed by the claim that it was common in the speech of cultivated Americans.

This response reminds us that people do look to dictionaries for guidance of this kind; to fail to offer such warnings is clearly unhelpful. Whether we agree with this attitude or not, it clearly speaks to a wider public disapproval of this word; despite its treatment by Webster's *Third*, more than forty years on *ain't* is still considered unacceptable in correct usage. The continued stigmatization of this word is particularly striking given that it was frequently used by upper-class speakers in England—such as Dorothy L. Sayers' fictional detective Lord Peter Wimsey—in the nineteenth and twentieth centuries.

In his *Modern English Usage* of 1926, H. W. Fowler expressed his disappointment that, since it functioned as a natural contraction of *am not I*, *ain't* should be frowned upon. Fowler suspected that 'the shamefaced reluctance' with which speakers resorted to *am not I*, betrayed their 'sneaking affection for the *ain't I* that he (or still more she) fears will convict him of low breeding'. Notice how Fowler identifies the concern with *ain't* with questions of class and gender. Yet, in spite of Fowler's support for this natural contraction, Oxford Dictionaries online continues to warn its readers that *ain't* 'does not form part of standard English and should never be used in formal or written contexts'.

Rather than placing the authority in a single editor, the *American Heritage Dictionary* draws upon the expert judgements of a Usage Panel, comprising some two hundred authors, journalists, editors, and academics, who issue adjudications on questions of pronunciation, meaning, and usage, which feed into the dictionary's usage labels. In his preface to the dictionary Steven Pinker sums up the dictionary's policy with regard to the verdicts of its Usage Panel with the bold claim: 'The Usage Panel is always right.'

While the combined authority of this distinguished panel is certainly considerable, one wonders whether all the dictionary's users would concur with this statement. As chair of the Usage Panel, Pinker is well-placed to observe its workings; though, at the same time, he is perhaps least well-placed to offer a disinterested view of the authority of its judgements.

Academies

The desire to place such decisions in the hands of an authoritative committee has its roots in the concept of the linguistic academy—a governing body that makes pronouncements about correct usage. Such a council, known as L'Académie Française, was established for the French language by Cardinal Richelieu in 1635. The Académie remains responsible for regulating the French language today, issuing edicts governing acceptable usage as determined by its body of forty académiciens, known as the 'immortals'. Proposals to found a similar legislative body for the English language have been made in the past, though these have never been implemented.

In 1664 the Royal Society established a committee tasked with 'improving' the English language. In a series of meetings, its members, which included John Dryden and John Evelyn, debated the desirability and remit of an English Academy along the lines of that established in France. The discussions came to nothing, though the idea of an academy did not disappear.

In an essay of 1697 Daniel Defoe called upon King William III to set up an academy 'to polish and refine the English Tongue', and to establish a 'Purity and Propriety of Stile, and to purge it from all the Irregular Additions that Ignorance and Affectation have introduc'd.' Membership of this academy would be drawn from gentlemen and members of the nobility, whose natural authority would discourage the coining of unlicensed words, which would be criminalized in the same manner as false currency.

Defoe's suggestion received further impetus from Jonathan Swift in his 'Proposal for Correcting, Improving and Ascertaining the English Tongue' (1712). Swift objected to the way the English language was being corrupted by the many 'Abuses' and 'Absurdities' inflicted upon it by play-wrights, court fops, half-witted poets, university boys, and scribblers. He exhorted his putative academy to ignore custom and practice, which is tainted by 'gross Improprieties'; the committee's remit should be to root out words which deserve to be ejected, correct others, and revive some which have fallen out of use.

For Swift, the key task of such an academy would be to stabilize and fix the English language, preventing it from further change: 'It is better a Language should not be wholly perfect, than that it should be perpetually changing.' Similar developments were proposed in the USA, though with a comparable lack of success. John Adams, a future president, wrote a letter to Congress in 1780, proposing the establishment of an academy for 'refining, correcting, improving, and ascertaining the English language', which fell on deaf ears.

Perhaps the closest England has come to having an insti-tutionalized academy is the Society for Pure English, founded in 1913 by the poet Robert Bridges, who was con-cerned by the 'advancing decay' of English caused by the laziness of its speakers. Bridges attracted an impressive num-ber of distinguished academic supporters for his mission to improve the language as an aid for 'the intercommunication of ideas'. Yet, alongside his desire to promote intercultural harmony was a darker purpose that sought to root out the 'blundering corruptions' caused by those 'communities of other-speaking races' whose imperfect acquisition of the English language was infecting and mutilating the superior tongue. Bridges' conflicted aims demonstrate how attempts to purify and control English are often driven by social, moral, and racial agendas; by seeking to keep English pure, Bridges was really concerned with the purity of its speakers.

Calls for a governing body of the English language continue to be voiced today. In 2010, the Queen's English Society proposed the establishment of an Academy to establish 'a clear standard of good, correct, proper English'. While some journalists welcomed the stated aims, many questioned the credentials of the self-appointed committee members: 'by what authority would they sit in judgment?' asked David Mitchell, writing in *The Observer*.

All such proposals share a desire to invest authority in the hands of a small, selected minority, who would have the power to issue pronouncements about correct and incorrect usage. But, while ostensibly concerned with a common good—the future health of the English language—there is always a personal agenda lurking behind such proposals. While directing his anxieties at the future of the English nation and its language, Swift's proposal reveals a concern that a changing language would result in his own works becoming unintelligible to subsequent generations. Despite espousing a common goal, these proposals are beset by personal linguistic prejudice that undermines any possibility of agreeing a shared set of linguistic norms. Where Swift chastised the pronunciation of the court, this was precisely the variety that had been endorsed and recommended as a model by earlier writers.

Usage Guides

If dictionaries cannot be trusted to provide the kind of prescriptive authority that people seek, and without an academy of distinguished scholars to draw upon, where should we look for reliable and authoritative linguistic pronouncements? An alternative source to the dictionary is the usage guide, which tends to adopt a more prescriptive approach and which focuses on a small subset of frequently disputed points of usage. But where we might turn to such a guide in search of a single, unassailable viewpoint, the reality is a wealth of conflicting advice in a range of publications.

The most successful and long-lasting of such guides is undoubtedly H. W. Fowler's *Modern English Usage* (1926), beloved of language purists in search of unambiguously prescriptive statements (see Figure 7). Fowler was a Classics teacher who turned to lexicography, working on the first editions of the *Concise Oxford Dictionary* (1911) and *Pocket Oxford Dictionary* (1929). *Modern English Usage* grew out of a usage guide that he co-wrote with his brother Frank, *The King's English* (1906); some of its entries—'Shall & Will', 'On Hyphens', 'Split Infinitives', 'Fused Participles'—were issued as tracts intended to provide guidance for writers by the Society for Pure English. But while Fowler's approach reflected the prescriptive attitude of his time, he was also conscious of the importance of usage, or what he referred to as 'idiom' (see Box 3).

There is a continual tug-of-war between these two sides to Fowler's approach—a desire to observe and record on the one hand, an impulse to regulate and prescribe on the other hand. That Fowler was aware of the paradox at the heart of his enterprise can be seen in his entry on *that* and *which*: 'What grammarians say should be has perhaps less influence

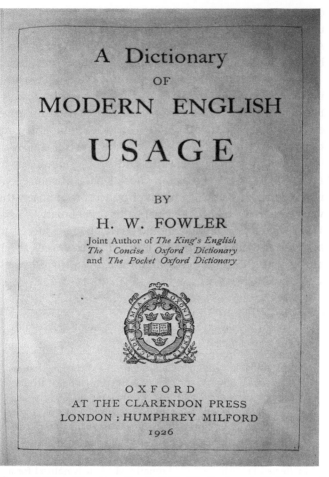

Figure 7 The ultimate authority? H. W. Fowler, *A Dictionary of Modern English Usage* (1926), title page.

on what shall be than even the more modest of them realize; usage evolves itself little disturbed by their likes and dislikes. And yet the temptation to show how better use might have been made of the material to hand is sometimes irresistible.'

Fowler's suspicion that his prescriptions would have little impact on future behaviour is partly borne out by history; the *Oxford English Dictionary* revision to *literally* discussed earlier runs entirely counter to Fowler's attempt to curb this erroneous usage: 'We have come to such a pass with this emphasizer that where the truth would require us to insert with a strong expression "not literally, of course, but in a manner of speaking", we do not hesitate to insert the very word that we ought to be at pains to repudiate.'

But against such failures should be weighed his success in bringing attention to various contested areas of usage, such as the distinctions between *will* and *shall*, *different from* vs.

BOX 3 *H. W. Fowler,* Modern English Usage *(1926). From the entry for 'Idiom'*

....

'In this book, "an idiom" is any form of expression that, as compared with other forms in which the principles of abstract grammar, if there is such a thing, would have allowed the idea in question to be clothed, has established itself as the particular way preferred by Englishmen & therefore presumably characteristic of them. "Idiom" is the sum total of such forms of expression, & is consequently the same as natural or racy or unaffected English; that is idiomatic which it is natural for a normal Englishman to say or write.'

---

different to, owing to vs. *due to*, which continue to influence popular usage today.

Fowler's work was revised by Ernest Gowers in a second edition of 1965, and a more radical revision and updating appeared in 1996, under the editorship of R. W. Burchfield. As a former editor of the *Oxford English Dictionary*, Burchfield brought a descriptive approach to the task, recasting many of Fowler's prescriptions in light of established precedent. The third edition was strongly criticized by many reviewers who felt let down by Burchfield's more permissive stance. Readers viewed Burchfield's passive acceptance of the misuses that had become so prevalent as a dereliction of duty; rather than predicting that today's errors would become acceptable tomorrow, Burchfield should be fighting to preserve standards of correctness. A reviewer of 'Thoroughly Modern Burchfield' in the American journal *New Criterion* wrote: 'It would be better for Burchfield to be proved wrong by the future than to prove a doormat in the present. The future might even turn out different if the Burchfields of this world took a more courageously combative stand.'

The recent publication of a fourth edition of Fowler's *A Dictionary of Modern English Usage* (2015), edited by Jeremy Butterfield, testifies to the durability of the brand as well as the marketability of the prescriptive approach. While the guide itself offers a reasoned account of different attitudes to variant usages, an article in *The Guardian* newspaper publicizing the volume adopted a much more openly partisan stance. Here Butterfield rails against those who pronounce the letter 'aitch' as 'haitch': 'The eighth letter of the alphabet is pronounced "aitch". Look it up in a dictionary if you don't believe me. I challenge you to find an "h" sound in the pronunciation shown there. People born from the 1980s onwards apparently favour this pronunciation; youth is no excuse for illiteracy.'

If, however, you follow Butterfield's advice and look up 'haitch' in the dictionary he himself has edited, you find an explicit recognition that the pronunciation of the letter 'h' as 'haitch' has long been considered perfectly acceptable in UK dialects. The entry claims that this pronunciation is often considered 'unspeakably uncouth' by older RP speakers, but this is simply a recognition of the prejudices and ignorance of such speakers, who consider regional speech to be inferior to their own.

The prescriptive usage guide has enjoyed a longer life-span in the USA; the American equivalent to Fowler is Strunk and White's *The Elements of Style*. Based upon a work first published in 1920 by William Strunk Jr, *The Elements of Style* was updated and expanded by E. B. White (author of children's favourites *Charlotte's Web* and *Stuart Little*) in 1959. The work has appeared in three further editions and has sold over ten million copies since its first appearance. In 2011, *Time* magazine included 'Strunk and White' in its list of the hundred most influential non-fiction books published since the magazine's foundation in 1923. The longevity of this publication, even in the UK, is well demonstrated by the recent success of *Gwynne's Grammar*, nearly half of which is a straight reprint of the original *The Elements of Style*.

A common feature of usage guides is a tendency to issue *ipse dixit* (literally 'he himself said it') prescriptions, based upon little more than personal preference. Given the idio-syncrasy of their judgements, it is common to find such authorities differing in their pronouncements. In such cases, how are we to determine who is correct?

An example of such disagreement concerns the choice between the adverbs *first* and *firstly* when enumerating a list of points: should one write 'first break the eggs, secondly add the sugar, thirdly beat the mixture', or should it be 'firstly break the eggs', and so on? H. W. Fowler prefers *firstly* in such contexts, describing the insistence upon *first* in strikingly tolerant terms as 'one of the harmless pedantries in which those who like oddities because they are odd are free to indulge, provided that they abstain from censuring those who do not share the liking'. But, while there may appear a logic to such claims, since there is a clear symmetry to *firstly*, *secondly*, *thirdly*, Neville Gwynne rejects Fowler's dismissal of *first* as 'outrageous', calling upon an alternative authority: Eric Partridge's *Usage and Abusage* (1942), which states categorically, 'Firstly is inferior to first, even when secondly, thirdly, follow it'.

Typical of such debates is an absolute conviction in the correctness of one's own position, even when it is at odds with that of other authorities to whom one defers on other occasions, as Gwynne frequently does with Fowler. At the core of such debates is a belief that, where two or more variants exist, there can be one and only one correct form. But this assumption could be questioned: if *first* is perfectly acceptable, does that necessarily require *firstly* to be wrong? Might not both *first* and *firstly* be equally acceptable variants?

Sources

Another way of determining acceptability is to turn to examples of actual usage. Dr Johnson was the first lexicographer to include citations to illustrate uses of the words he defined. But Johnson was confessedly prescriptive in his choice of the sources from which he extracted these citations, preferring to restrict himself to writers whose works he considered to preserve the 'pure sources of genuine diction'.

Johnson saw a close link between *authority* and *author*; correct usage should be based upon the examples of great literary writers: Shakespeare, Milton, and Spenser. Since the selection of which literary authorities to choose was made by Johnson himself, albeit drawing upon an established canon, he was thereby introducing his own subjective opinions via an alternative route, while simultaneously appearing to ground his lexicographical judgements in an objective authority.

For many of his readers, however, Johnson's work provided the guarantee of authority they were seeking. On publication, Johnson's initially reluctant patron, Lord Chesterfield, submitted himself entirely to its judgements: 'I hereby declare that I make a total surrender of all my rights and privileges in the English language, as a freeborn British subject, to the said Mr Johnson, during the term of his dictatorship.' But not all Johnson's readers were quite so subservient. When challenged by a lady at a dinner party about his erroneous definition of *pastern* as 'the knee of an horse', Johnson was forced to admit that it was due to 'ignorance, pure ignorance'. (The pastern is properly the part between the fetlock and hoof.)

The dictionary's fiercest critic, however, was Johnson himself. Despite having grounded his work in authoritative usage, he remained sceptical of its potential to preserve the purity of the tongue. Although he embarked on this task with hopes of fixing the language and preventing further change, he later recognized the folly of trying to 'enchain syllables' and 'lash the wind'.

The first edition of the *Oxford English Dictionary* (published under its original title of *The New English Dictionary on Historical Principles* and issued in a series of fascicules from 1884 to 1928) differed from previous works in being a historical dictionary. Instead of simply documenting contemporary usage, the *OED* set out to chart the history of English vocabulary from Old English to the present day. Included in each entry are large numbers of quotations from its sources, illustrating changes in spelling, meaning, and usage over time. To enable coverage of this vast historical spectrum, the *OED* editors relied upon the efforts of an extensive volunteer reading programme. In 1879, the editor, James Murray, issued an appeal to the English-speaking and English-reading public, calling for volunteers to submit instances of individual words across a whole range of published works. The call received some 800 British and 500 American responses; contributors included renowned scholars but also retired army officers, schoolteachers, clergymen, housewives, and, in Dr W. C. Minor—one of the most prolific—a convicted murderer and inmate of Broadmoor psychiatric hospital. In total, these volunteer readers supplied over a million citations in the years running up to the publication of the first instalment.

But while the coverage this enabled was considerably more inclusive than that of Dr Johnson, it remained necessarily limited and partial. More significantly, the *OED* has tended to perpetuate the prominence of great literary writers such as Shakespeare, whose works were exhaustively mined for inclusion. Since Shakespeare, Chaucer, and Milton were viewed as foundational to the formation of English literature, it seemed natural to the *OED* readers and editors that their works should be fully recorded in the dictionary's entries. The validity of this procedure was apparently endorsed by the completed dictionary, which showed that Shakespeare and Chaucer were indeed the earliest cited authors for many innovative usages. But this is circular reasoning: since their works had been privileged in the making of the dictionary, it was inevitable that the dictionary should endorse their linguistic importance.

The ongoing third edition (published online in instalments) draws upon a much more diverse collection of texts; while the reading programme continues today, *OED* editors also draw upon a huge electronic corpus—a searchable collection of texts in electronic format. This corpus, currently standing at 2.5 billion words, comprises texts spanning a variety of genres and media: literary works, magazines, newspapers, journals, blogs, websites, and emails. Where earlier editions of the *OED* tended to focus on the English of the British Isles, the Oxford corpus includes texts from all over the English-speaking world.

Despite this, the legacy of the privileging of canonical writers in the original dictionary continues to loom large. Even though this large-scale revision of the dictionary has been underway since 2000, Figure 8 reveals that Shakespeare remains the second most-quoted author (after *The Times* newspaper), while Chaucer is placed at number 6, and Milton at number 7.

The importance of the canon of great literary writers continues to influence debates over correct usage today. Appealing to such precedents remains a common tactic among writers seeking an authoritative basis upon which to sanction or outlaw a particular usage. Especially common is recourse to the works of Shakespeare or the Authorized Version of the Bible (1611), considered to be two of the great monuments of the English language.

In 'Politics and the English Language' (1945), George Orwell satirized contemporary prose style by contrasting

Top 1000 sources in the OED

Search within top 1000 sources: Enter search

Click a column header to change the sort order of the table: click again to reverse sort.

# Name	Dates	Total number of quotations	First evidence for word	First evidence for sense
1. Times	1788–	39984	1684	7724
2. William Shakespeare	1564–1616	33118	1523	7792
3. Walter Scott	1771–1832	17084	430	2148
4. Philosophical Transactions	1665–	13514	1665	5414
5. Encyclopaedia Britannica	1768–	14304	830	2017
6. Geoffrey Chaucer	c1340–1400	13403	1990	5415
7. John Milton	1608–1674	12406	589	2035
8. Cursor Mundi	c1400–1450	11798	1050	3241
9. Nature	1869–	11882	732	1983

My entries (0)

My searches (0)

The top one thousand authors and works cited in the OED

The Sources page provides details about the most frequently quoted authors or works in the OED.

Search for an author or title using the search box, or select an author name or work title for more information and links to dictionary entries.

Sources can be sorted in various ways by selecting the column headings.

Get more help.

Figure 8 List of top sources cited in the *Oxford English Dictionary*, 3rd edition.

it with that of the Authorized Version. To demonstrate modern writers' tendency to overuse polysyllabic loanwords, Orwell placed a verse from the Authorized Version alongside his own parodic rendering of the same text into Modern English (see Box 4).

Rather more playfully, Mark Forsyth, author of the bestselling *Etymologicon*, proposes two methods of determining the acceptability of a contested usage. The first is to apply the SWANS test (Sounds Wrong to a Native Speaker) and the second the GAS test (God and Shakespeare): does the construction appear in the works of Shakespeare or in the Authorized Version of the Bible?

Attempts to make pronouncements about contemporary usage founded on the language of Shakespeare and the

---

BOX 4 *George Orwell's rendering of Ecclesiastes chapter 9, verse 11, into Modern English*
....

Authorized Version:

I returned, and saw under the sun, that the race is not to the swift, nor the battle to the strong, neither yet bread to the wise, nor yet riches to men of understanding, nor yet favour to men of skill; but time and chance happeneth to them all.

Orwell's version:

Objective consideration of contemporary phenomena compels the conclusion that success or failure in competitive activities exhibits no tendency to be commensurate with innate capacity, but that a considerable element of the unpredictable must invariably be taken into account.

Authorized Version of the Bible fail to take account of the fact that these works were produced in the early seventeenth century. Since Standard English no longer uses *doth*, *ye*, *thou*, and *methinks*, it hardly seems relevant to hold up such texts as guides to modern usage.

Shakespeare's language is creative and innovative, producing many words and idioms that are no longer acceptable in Modern English; by contrast, the Authorized Version consciously adopted a markedly conservative form of the language, preserving the 'eth' endings on third singular present-tense verbs, and employing earlier *his* instead of *its* ('If the salt have lost his savour'), which would have sounded old-fashioned even to its first readers.

Shakespeare's usage has not always held the authority it has today. Rather than viewing Shakespeare's works as a model of correctness, eighteenth-century editors frequently emended his texts to ensure that they conformed to contemporary grammatical standards. For instance, Shakespeare made frequent use of the double comparative and double superlative: 'To some more fitter place' (*Measure for Measure*), 'This was the most unkindest cut of all' (*Julius Caesar*). These constructions were condemned by eighteenth-century grammarians on grounds of logic: since it was impossible to have degrees of comparative and superlative, such constructions must be incorrect.

The poet and dramatist John Dryden was an especially vocal critic of the grammatical sloppiness he encountered in the works of supposed great writers like Shakespeare and Ben Jonson, claiming that every page contained some

'Solecism of Speech' or 'notorious flaw in Sence'. Rather than view Shakespeare's use of these constructions as evidence for their acceptability, eighteenth-century editors such as Alexander Pope simply removed them; in Pope's edition these lines read: 'To some more fitting place' and 'This, this was the unkindest cut of all'.

Logic

This eighteenth-century prioritizing of logic over historical usage retains an appeal for some grammarians today. In the preface to *Gwynne's Grammar*, N. M. Gwynne insists that, in formulating his prescriptions, he is not relying upon his own judgements, but rather on logic. For Gwynne, English grammar is 'not a haphazard collection of rules that (a) happen to have been put together over the centuries, and (b) happen to exist in their present form at this point of time in our history. The rules always have a *logic* underpinning them.' As we have seen, the idea that correctness can be determined by applying the rules of logic is not a new one, but we might question whether it can legitimately be applied to language.

One grammatical feature that is often stigmatized on grounds of illogicality is the double negative. Its opponents argue that constructions such as 'I didn't get no answer' are self-evidently wrong, since they imply the opposite of what they attempt to say: that is, not getting no answer logically means that you did get an answer. Simon Heffer counsels the readers of his *Strictly English* (2011) to 'Avoid double negatives. They are offences against logic and, if they are an attempt at being funny, they fail.'

But, while this may be a valid argument according to logic, or the rules of mathematics—where two negatives do indeed make a positive—is it appropriate to apply such strictures to language? Surely no speaker who heard the construction 'I didn't steal no car' would understand it as a confession; the use of the double negative would be taken to function as an intensifier—just as it was intended by the speaker— vehemently denying an accusation. When we hear Mick Jagger of the Rolling Stones sing 'I can't get no satisfaction', we do not respond with: 'Well, if you're perfectly satisfied what are you complaining about'; we understand this to be an intensified statement of dissatisfaction.

Human language is not like a computer language, where every value must be either positive or negative; language allows for many more complex gradations than are possible in a simple binary system. We can see that the mathematical model fails if we try it on a sentence with a triple negative. If it is true that double negatives cancel each other out, such sentences should be negative. But, if that is so, which negative remains? Take the sentence: 'I didn't tell nobody nothing'. Does this mean 'I told somebody nothing', or 'I didn't tell somebody something'?

Like many rules that are apparently based on logic, the view that double negatives are illogical is an artificial rule introduced in the eighteenth century. It first appears in James Greenwood's *An Essay Towards a Practical English Grammar* (1711), where we find the statement: 'Two Negatives, or two Adverbs of Denying, do in English affirm.'

As is usual in such works, no support for the claim is offered; it is certainly not based on practice, since double negatives had been common since Old English. A famous instance appears in Geoffrey Chaucer's description of the knight in the *Canterbury Tales*, who 'nevere yet no vileynye [evil] ne sayde... unto no maner wight [person].' Since there are four negatives here (*nevere, no, ne, no*) a prescriptivist might be inclined to claim that Chaucer is signalling the knight's rudeness, but this is self-evidently not the implication; the incremental build-up of negatives is intended to underline the knight's purity of speech and good manners.

This is not just a quirk of the English language; multiple negation as a form of reinforcement is found in other languages, like French, where 'je ne veux rien' uses both the negative *ne* and *rien* 'nothing'—'I don't want nothing'.

Where Dryden and Pope objected to Shakespeare's double comparatives and superlatives, modern usage pundits outlaw the treatment of words like *perfect* and *unique* as gradable adjectives on grounds of logic. H. W. Fowler claimed: 'It is nonsense to call anything *more, most, very, somewhat, rather,* or *comparatively unique*.' In *The King's English* (1999), Kingsley Amis denounced this 'misuse', which he considered to be 'notorious among the almost-literate'. Simon Heffer agrees: 'To argue that something is *more* unique, or that it is the most unique in the world is literally meaningless. Scarcely less vacuous are phrases like *almost unique* or *nearly unique*. Something is either unique or it is not.'

But, while it is true that *unique* has a core meaning which descends from a mathematically precise sense 'one of a kind', deriving from its origin in the Latin *unus* 'one', the word is commonly used in a secondary, looser sense of 'unusual'. While it is clearly impossible to have gradations of uniqueness in the primary sense 'one of a kind', it is perfectly acceptable to write more or less unique in the sense 'unusual'.

Etymology

But if correctness cannot be discerned by logic, how should it be determined? One answer is that it should be defined by history; older, established usages are surely more correct than newer innovations. This was certainly the view of the ancients who coined the term *etymology*, which is derived from the Greek *etumos* 'true', and referred to a word's primary, or true, meaning. But, if we were to apply such a concept to the majority of common English words today, this would result in considerable confusion; the word *silly* is first recorded in the sense 'pious', *nice* meant 'foolish', and *buxom* meant 'obedient'.

Dr Johnson was attracted by the logic of such an approach when he embarked on his dictionary, referring to etymology as the 'natural and primitive signification' of a word. But experience led him to recognize the fallacy of this approach, as is apparent from the illustration he included in the entry for *etymology*: 'When words are restrained, by common usage, to a particular sense, to run up to etymology, and construe them by Dictionaries, is wretchedly ridiculous'. H. W. Fowler was similarly aware of the limitations of this view, noting that, while etymology is an interesting subject of study for its own ends, it is not a valid means for understanding how words should be used today.

Yet this approach is still urged by usage pundits, who insist on preserving the etymological senses of words such as *aggravate* (make worse), *decimate* (reduction by ten per cent), *dilemma* (choice between *two* propositions), and *chronic* (long-lasting). But where modern pundits argue that the supposed misuses are the result of contemporary sloppiness, the evidence shows them to be much more established; the first recorded use of *aggravate* to mean 'irritate' dates from the sixteenth century.

The difficulty of enforcing such restrictions becomes apparent when we observe that even those advocating such semantic restrictions struggle to observe them. In *The King's English*, Kingsley Amis insisted on the distinction between the noun *enormity* 'great wickedness' and its adjective *enormous* 'very large'; he wrote sniffily of T. S. Eliot's erroneous reference to the 'enormity of man's ignorance'. But in Amis' novel *Lucky Jim*, we find the hero Jim Dixon, confronted with the ordeal of delivering a lecture on Merrie England, panting a little 'with the enormity of it'.

Who is correct here? Amis the usage pundit, or Amis the writer? As is often the case, when we turn to the evidence of etymology, the waters get murkier rather than clearer. *Enormity* and *enormous* are from the same Latin root, *ex* 'out of' + *norma* 'norm, rule', which entered English via the French word *énormité*. Up until the eighteenth century, both words were used in the sense of 'abnormal', 'non-standard', 'irregular', whether referring to behaviour or to size. It was only then that an artificial distinction was introduced between *enormity* and *enormousness*. So, while this distinction has historical authority, it is not a distinction that can be traced back to the words' origins; it is rather an eighteenth-century attempt to regulate usage by constructing an artificial rule.

To judge from etymology, then, it is perfectly correct to use *enormity* to refer to size, just as it would also be acceptable to use *enormous* to refer to a great wickedness. Despite this, even Barack Obama came under fire from the usage police when he alluded humbly to the enormity of the task ahead in his presidential acceptance speech in 2008. The newly elected president was castigated by the press for this apparent howler; and it was also cited by Simon Heffer in his *Strictly English*, where he maintains that 'one should speak not of the *enormity* of the task, but of its *enormousness*: even if one is President of the United States.' Yet in his own life of Thomas Carlyle, *Moral Desperado*, Heffer writes: 'He was about to embark on his first large-scale literary project, a life of Schiller, and was overwhelmed by the enormity of the task.' Such standards are evidently easier to police than they are to observe.

Descriptive or Prescriptive?

The tension between descriptive and prescriptive attitudes that are at the centre of the issues discussed in this chapter is not easily resolved. While lexicographers continue to insist that the dictionaries they produce should not be seen as a guide to correct usage, that is precisely how many people use them.

Even as they renounce such authority, dictionary makers recognize the commercial value of this market. In the preface to the third edition of the *OED*, its editor dismisses the myth that the dictionary is a comprehensive account of all English words and their meanings, since such coverage would be impossible. But it is understandable how such myths continue to be propagated, since the dictionary's own homepage carries the strapline: 'the definitive record of the English language'.

While lexicographers justify their inclusion of new words on the grounds of their wide use, it is surely significant that updates that include controversial new words are more likely to generate headlines than mundane ones. In 2014, Collins' dictionary became the first to allow Twitter users to vote on which words were included in its next update—a contest that resulted in the inclusion of *adorkable*. Is this evidence of a shift in authority from the lexicographers to its community of users? Or is this just a clever marketing stunt by a company seeking to extend its online presence and to exploit its advertising potential?

Placing authority in the readers' hands is a feature of online dictionaries such as *Wiktionary* and *Urban Dictionary*. Here the community of users is responsible for supplying definitions and quotations, as well as choosing which words are included. Where modern print dictionaries aim to supply neutral definitions that report the facts of contemporary usage, *Urban Dictionary*'s contributions frequently reflect the subjective bias and personal prejudices of its users. The *Urban Dictionary* entry for *adorkable* presents a lengthy definition from a candidly personal perspective: 'The best kind of guys! A guy that is a nerd, but in a very cute/adorable way that is very attractive. They are not afraid to be themselves and are usually very sweet, smart, and have the best sense of humor once you get to know them. Best of all, they know how to treat a girl well and appreciate her. Plus, they are really good to have around when the computer breaks.'

This form of definition returns to a Johnsonian approach, where personal opinions and prejudices are openly offered; compare, for example, Johnson's definition of *patron*, a blatant dig at the dilatoriness of Lord Chesterfield's support: 'One who countenances, supports or protects. Commonly a wretch who supports with insolence, and is paid with flattery.'

While the subjectivity of such definitions is immediately apparent, in other cases such partisanship can be harder to spot, especially where it is apparently justified with reference to authority or to history. But, since there is no single linguistic authority, it is impossible to make such an appeal without allowing some degree of personal bias and prejudice to creep in. References to history, or the 'genius' of the language, similarly fail, since this is simply an unwillingness to recognize that today's rules are the result of normative determinations that were established at earlier periods in the history of English.

Those who object to the use of *they* as a singular pronoun appeal to history as justification for the employment of the masculine pronoun *he* to include the feminine pronoun *she*. Casting this 'abominable' use of *they* as a recent fad—'an attempt made in the last century or so'—Simon Heffer insists upon a preference for 'the old rule that "the masculine will be taken to include the feminine wherever necessary"'. But by casting this use of *they* as a newfangled illiteracy imposed upon the language by the pressures of political correctness, while appealing to an old rule—placed in quotation marks as if to imply it is taken from some unnamed authoritative source—Heffer misrepresents the linguistic evidence. The use of *they*, *their*, and *them* to refer to a singular subject of indeterminate gender can be traced back to the Middle Ages, and has been used by many canonical literary writers, including Shakespeare.

The outlawing of singular *they* to which Heffer appeals is the result of a linguistic prescription of the nineteenth century—a period of male dominance that viewed the treatment of masculine gender as a default position as unexceptional. To adopt without question the grammatical rules that were codified in the past is tacitly to accept these concomitant prejudices and assumptions.

As a more extreme example we might consider Thomas Wilson's insistence, in his grammatical handbook *Arte of Rhetorique* (1553), that a male subject should always precede a female one, thereby maintaining a 'natural order': 'Some will set the carte before the horse, as thus. My mother and my father are both at home, euen as thoughe the good man of the house ware no breaches . . . let vs kepe a natural order, and set the man before the woman for maners sake.'

While the active promotion of inclusive forms of address, such as the recent coinage *Mx*, is often dismissed as a misguided effort to pervert the natural development of the language, such attempts are no more artificial than the kinds of deliberate interference carried out in the eighteenth and nineteenth centuries. Yet the notion that the processes of standardization and codification of the past are of a different order from those of today can even trip up professional linguists. When the Linguistics Association of Great Britain proposed a motion to amend its constitution by renaming the chairman as the chairperson and removing generic masculine pronouns, it was voted down by its members on the grounds that linguists, whose role is to observe and describe language, should not be seen engaging in prescriptive practices.

Despite the many controversies that we have identified in this chapter concerning correct usage and how it should be established, each of the authorities discussed would agree that there is a single authoritative form of the language, known as Standard English. But how did this situation arise? Where did Standard English come from, how did it come to win such widespread acceptance in the face of so much disagreement, and what is its status today? These are the questions to be addressed in Chapter 4.

4

Standards

In Chapter 2 we traced the history of the English language, from its beginnings to the present-day. But this was essentially a history of just one form of English, Standard English: the dominant form of the language today. Standard English is the variety taught to children in schools, used in prestigious institutions such as the government, the law, the BBC, and the language of the printed medium. It is a fixed variety, intolerant of variation, and is used throughout the population of English users, irrespective of geography.

However accustomed we may be to this situation, it is an artificial one, since human language is naturally prone to variation and change. We can see this if we consider only the spoken language, which exists in numerous different dialects spoken across Britain and the English-speaking world. These varieties of English vary in terms of their pronunciation (accent), grammar, and vocabulary. Standard English is simply one such dialect, albeit one which has been accorded a much higher social status than any other.

Despite this, many people today insist that Standard English is inherently superior. Such a view implies a misunderstanding of a standard language, which is simply an agreed norm that is selected in order to facilitate communication. We might compare Standard English with other modern standards, such as systems of currency, weights and measures, or voltage. No one system is inherently better than another; the benefit is derived from the general adoption of an established set of norms.

Another useful analogy is with the rules of the road. There is no reason why driving on the left (as in England) should be preferred over driving on the right-hand side (as on the continent and in the USA). The key reason to choose one over another is to ensure that everyone is driving on the same side of the road.

The application of the adjective *standard* to refer to language is first recorded in the eighteenth century, a development of its earlier use to refer to classical literature. A desire to associate English literature with the Classics prompted a wish to see the English language achieve a standard form. This ambition was most clearly articulated by Jonathan Swift: 'But the English Tongue is not arrived to such a degree of Perfection, as to make us apprehend any Thoughts of its Decay; and if it were once refined to a certain Standard, perhaps there might be Ways found out to fix it forever' (*A Proposal for Correcting, Improving and Ascertaining the English Tongue*, 1712). By the nineteenth century, the term Standard English referred specifically to a prestige variety, spoken only by the upper classes, yet viewed as a benchmark against which the majority of native English speakers were measured and accused of using their language incorrectly.

The identification of Standard English with the elite classes was overtly drawn by H. C. Wyld, one of the most influential academic linguists of the first half of the twentieth century. Despite embarking on his philological career as a neutral observer, for whom one variety was just as valuable as another, Wyld's later work clearly identified Standard English as the sole acceptable form of usage: 'It may be called Good English, Well-bred English, Upper-class English.' These applications of the phrase Standard English reveal a telling shift from the sense of standard signalling 'in general use' (as in the phrase 'standard issue') to the sense of a level of quality (as in the phrase 'to a high standard').

From this we may discern that Standard English is a relatively recent phenomenon, which grew out of an eighteenth-century anxiety about the status of English, and which prompted a concern for the codification and 'ascertaining', or fixing, of English. Before the eighteenth century, dialect variation was the norm, both in speech and in writing.

Standard English: What It Is and What It Isn't

In defining a standard language, it is useful to begin by highlighting what it isn't. For instance, the distinction between standard and non-standard English does not correlate with the difference between formal and colloquial usage. It is perfectly possible to speak casually using Standard English, to employ taboo words—so-called 'bad language'—without flouting the grammatical principles of Standard English. Similarly, it is also theoretically possible to speak Standard English in any accent, since accent refers only to features of pronunciation, whereas dialect encompasses vocabulary and grammar as well. It is more likely, however, that speakers using broad local accents will employ features of grammar and vocabulary characteristic of their local dialect.

Although there is widespread agreement that there is such a thing as Standard English today, there is considerable confusion as to exactly what this label represents. Such confusion commonly stems from a failure to distinguish between social and linguistic factors. A linguistic definition of Standard English focuses on its intolerance of variation and insistence on fixity. Since the function of a standard language is to aid communication over a wide geographical area, allowing variation would clearly be dysfunctional. Regional variation found in Middle English could be tolerated because during that period written English functioned as a purely local language; communication on a national level was handled in French and Latin.

Another functional aspect of a standard language is that it is 'elaborated', so that it becomes the variety employed for a range of different linguistic functions. Standard English is used by the government, legal, and educational systems, which all help to reinforce and sustain its continued acceptance as the single acceptable form of written English.

The association of Standard English with these various institutions lends it prestige, so that it has become the variety that people associate with social advancement. Success in the education system and access to the prestigious professions require a competence in the handling of Standard English. As a consequence it is this variety that is taught in schools, though there remains much debate about the extent to which Standard English should be allowed to dominate over local forms of English. Some educators consider it the job of teachers to replace all dialect use with Standard English, whereas others support the tolerance of dialect. Since dialect is closely linked to identity, attempts to eradicate its use among children run the risk of being both culturally and psychologically damaging.

Because of its status as a superposed variety, Standard English is unique among the various dialects of English in having social prestige, leading many people to view it as coterminous with the English language itself. Those who do not use Standard English are frequently considered illiterate, and the variety they employ is viewed as inferior to the standard. But this dominance of Standard English is a consequence of its social elevation, not the result of any linguistic superiority. In popular usage, the term *dialect* is often employed to refer to a non-standard, or even substandard, form of the language. But for linguists the term *dialect* is neutral—Scouse English (the dialect of the city of Liverpool) and Standard English are simply two equivalent dialects, although ones with different social connotations.

In many cases, objections to regional dialect or accent have little to do with linguistic issues. More often, such judgements reflect social prejudice, which seeks to denigrate another person's speech simply because it is different to one's own. A YouGov poll carried out in 2014 asked British people which accent they found most attractive, though no explanation was offered as to what the criteria for an attractive accent might be. The highest ranked accents were Southern Irish, Received Pronunciation, and Welsh, while the 'ugliest' accents were Mancunian, Scouse, and Brummie (spoken respectively in the cities of Manchester, Liverpool, and Birmingham). An article in *The Mirror* newspaper carried the headline 'Sorry Brummies, the rest of the UK don't like you', exemplifying the way that having the right accent is closely linked with social acceptance. In another account of the report's findings, a journalist suggested that those who wish to impress their boss should consciously adopt BBC English, or even Irish English, openly advocating that the way people speak should be conditioned by the prejudices of their employers.

For others, the solution to such entrenched social prejudice is to ensure that children are alerted to the social disadvantages attached to regional varieties while in school. In his book *Does Accent Matter?* (1989), John Honey advised that children should be warned to expect that 'in the real world their accents may be used as an indicator of their origins, the extent of their educatedness, the system of values with which they identify and whether these are associated with a narrow local group or with the wider society'. But while local speech patterns are necessarily indicative of a person's origins, there is no intrinsic reason why they should be markers of their level of education, value system, and social position. Honey's proposal that such people ought to acquire Standard English to avoid such stigma is hardly the solution; why should dialect speakers be expected to shed their accent to avoid being subjected to social prejudice?

The respective roles of Standard English and local dialect in education were subject to public debate in 2013, when the head teacher of a school in Middlesbrough wrote to parents urging them to correct their children's use of improper phrases like 'I done that', 'Gizit 'ere', 'I dunno', 'It's nowt', pronunciations such as 'free fifteen' instead of 'three fifteen', and the plural pronoun *yous*. The head teacher explained that the letter was motivated by a desire to equip children for the workplace, where dialects can be seen as disadvantageous.

This controversial attempt to stamp out local dialect in the home won the support of many parents, who were in favour of the school's efforts to educate their children in Standard English. The letter was opposed by professional linguists, however, who argued that such an approach does not improve a child's command of the written standard, and has the potential to damage their social and educational development. Children use dialect to signal belonging within their peer groups, families, and local communities; to insist on the unacceptability of such forms in speech in the classroom runs the further risk of causing children to avoid asking and answering questions for fear of speaking 'incorrectly'.

Similar debates were sparked when the board of a school in Oakland, California, voted to change its policy regarding the education of African American children in Standard English. Given their consistently low level of achievement in the standard language, the board resolved to extend greater recognition to the vernacular spoken by the children themselves—a variety known to scholars as African American English (AAE), and more widely as Ebonics, a blend of *ebony* and *phonics*.

In proposing to use AAE as a bridge to the acquisition of Standard English, the Oakland board sought to recognize the difficulties experienced by Ebonics speakers who were being educated in a language very different from their own vernacular dialect. This legislation proved hugely contentious and received widespread condemnation in the press, which erroneously reported the board's proposal as a plan to view AAE as equivalent in status to Standard English. For many people this was seen as both unhelpful and insulting, consigning the children to a lifetime of underachievement. Some journalists were sympathetic to the motivation behind the decision, but questioned the strategy itself: if children are told that they are speaking a distinct language, why should they bother to acquire Standard English at all?

These examples underline the fact that—whatever our attitude towards non-standard dialects—schools have a duty to teach Standard English to children, irrespective of their background and linguistic heritage. Not to do so would be a dereliction of duty, since Standard English is an essential tool for enabling children to pass exams, and equipping them for the world of work.

Rather than simply ignoring differences between standard and dialectal forms of English, a better response would be to highlight them as a means of educating children in the diversity of English and its various functions. Teachers should aim to enable all pupils to read and write Standard English, but should also be tolerant of, even supportive of, the use of a non-standard variety in other contexts. Just as many European nationals grow up speaking more than one language, so English children can be encouraged to be 'bidialectal'—that is, to be able to use distinct dialects for different functions.

The head teacher of the Middlesbrough school appealed to the government's literacy framework in defence of her letter to parents, which requires children to write in Standard English. But the key word here is *write*—children can still be taught to write Standard English while being allowed to speak in their local dialect. Central to such an approach is the notion of 'appropriateness'—learning when it is permitted to use dialect and when only Standard English is acceptable.

Right Writing

Modern English spelling is the clearest example of an area of the language that has been fully standardized, though even here there remains room for variation and uncertainty. Should it be *judgement* or *judgment*, *yoghurt* or *yogurt*, *standardize* or *standardise*? If we compare Standard English spelling to that found in Middle English, we can see how far the process has advanced. Because there was no single standard variety of Middle English, dialects developed their own local spelling conventions. As a consequence, there were hundreds of variant spellings of common words like *through*, including *drowgh*, *yhurght*, *trghug*, and *trowffe*.

The process whereby this extensive variation was reduced to just one single correct spelling for most words can be traced back to the fifteenth century, when English began to replace Latin and French as a national language, creating a requirement for greater consistency in spelling. Another major factor in delivering a standard spelling system occurred later in the century, when William Caxton introduced the printing press and published the first books in English. Up to this point, books were written by hand (hence *manuscripts*) and were susceptible to both conscious and subconscious linguistic interference.

The technology of printing enabled the production of large numbers of copies of books with identical spelling. The advent of printing was also a factor in lowering the cost of books, which had the effect of raising literacy levels. Since printing workshops were initially located in Westminster, the London dialect used by the early printers was the variety encountered by readers throughout the country. But, while early printed books used a more consistent form of spelling than their handwritten predecessors, they continued to tolerate considerable variation.

This situation persisted for centuries, and it is not until the eighteenth century that we see a move towards complete fixity in the spelling of printed books. But, even after spelling had become fully standardized in print, non-standard spellings continued to be used in diaries, journals, private letters, and manuscripts. Even Dr Johnson, whose name has become synonymous with the fixing of the English language, employed non-standard spellings in his private writings. Johnson's *Dictionary* (1755) is also surprisingly tolerant of variation. He made no attempt to regulate between such pairs as *choak* and *choke* or *soap* and *sope*, and in cases like *complete* and *compleet* he even went to the trouble of inserting an entry under both spellings as an aid to his readers (see Box 5).

BOX 5   *From the Preface to Johnson's Dictionary of the English Language (1755)*

....

'In adjusting the ORTHOGRAPHY, which has been to this time unsettled and fortuitous, I found it necessary to distinguish those irregularities that are inherent in our tongue, and perhaps coeval with it, from others which the ignorance or negligence of later writers has produced. Every language has its anomalies, which, though inconvenient, and in themselves once unnecessary, must be tolerated among the imperfections of human things, and which require only to be registered, that they may not be increased, and ascertained, that they may not be confounded: but every language has likewise its improprieties and absurdities, which it is the duty of the lexicographer to correct or proscribe.'

Talking Proper

In the preface to his play *Pygmalion* (1912), George Bernard Shaw claimed that 'It is impossible for an Englishman to open his mouth without making some other Englishman hate or despise him.' This statement retains some truth today, since many people make judgements about a person's social background, education, personality, and even morality, based upon their accent.

But, despite the ubiquity of such views, the concept of better and worse accents is a relatively recent phenomenon. The earliest remarks about the social superiority of one accent over another appear in the sixteenth century. In a handbook for writers, *Arte of English Poesie* (1589), George

Puttenham advised his readers: 'Ye shall therefore take the vsuall speach of the Court, and that of London and the shires lying about London within lx [sixty] myles, and not much aboue.' Given the prominence of London and the court it is hardly surprising that Puttenham should identify its speech as the preferred accent for budding poets. But this is a social rather than a linguistic preference—an isolated remark made by a fourteenth-century chronicler promotes the midland dialect rather than that of the capital, on the grounds that it is more easily understood by speakers of both southern and northern dialects.

It was not until the second half of the eighteenth century that writers began to lament the variable state of English pronunciation, and to attempt to impose a fixed standard upon it. Since inconsistency in pronunciation was seen as being at the heart of the language's decline, a system of correct pronunciation was considered crucial to fixing the language and halting this downward trend. But, while the establishment of a standard accent was promoted in the cause of mutual understanding, the debate was driven more by a desire to align oneself with the correct group at a time of rapid social change.

It is no coincidence that the term *malapropism*—the ridiculous misuse of a word—was coined during this period of social and linguistic anxiety. The term is named after Mrs Malaprop, from the French phrase *mal à propos* 'inappropriate', a character in Richard Brinsley Sheridan's play *The Rivals* (1775), whose linguistic blunders include 'the very pineapple of politeness', 'my affluence is very small', and 'She's as headstrong as an allegory on the banks of the Nile'.

Where speaking incorrectly incurred social exclusion and humiliation, talking properly was a way of demonstrating membership of the most elite social circles. A provincial accent, in contrast, was seen as a barrier to entry to the most prestigious professions, such as the law and the church, where a refined and consistent delivery was considered essential.

The urge to codify usage led to the publication of numerous pronouncing dictionaries, beginning with *A General Dictionary of the English Language* (1780) by Thomas Sheridan, father of the playwright. Sheridan also delivered a hugely popular course of lectures on elocution, published in 1762. Sheridan's method was highly prescriptive; he is the first writer to comment negatively on the dropping of initial 'h'—a habit that continues to be highly stigmatized today. To counteract this unfortunate tendency, Sheridan proposed the following 'cure': 'Read over frequently all the words beginning with the letter H in the dictionary, and push them out with the full force of the breath 'till an habit is obtained of aspirating strongly.' Such methods anticipate the phonetic exercises to which Eliza Doolittle is subjected in the musical adaptation of Shaw's *Pygmalion*, *My Fair Lady* (1956), where she is made to repeat the phrase: 'In Hertford, Hereford, and Hampshire, hurricanes hardly ever happen'. But where Sheridan anticipated that the codification and promotion of a standard accent would contribute to national unity and remove prejudice, the result was the opposite.

Manuals of pronunciation continued to appear throughout the nineteenth century, helping to enshrine further the negative social and moral connotations of non-standard speech. Charles Dickens' novels draw abundantly upon the social embarrassment attached to marked features of a non-standard accent, including the dropping of 'h' stigmatized by Sheridan, as well as the use of certain proscribed pronunciations, such as *cowcumber* for *cucumber*, found in Mrs Gamp's speech in *Martin Chuzzlewit*: 'In case there should be such a thing as a cowcumber in the 'ouse, will you be so kind as bring it, for I'm rather partial to 'em, and they does a world of good in a sick room.'

From this emerged the concept of a received (in the sense 'generally accepted') pronunciation (RP)—a standard accent not limited to a particular dialect—a term first employed by the phonetician Alexander Ellis in 1869, who defined it as 'not widely differing in any particular locality, and admitting a certain degree of variety. It may be especially considered as the educated pronunciation of the metropolis, of the court, the pulpit and the bar.' It is striking that Ellis' RP is not a totally fixed entity, but rather a norm that tolerates internal variation depending upon locality. Ellis differed from his predecessors in refusing to make judgements as to the acceptability of particular pronunciations: 'As to the "correctness" or "impropriety" of such sounds I do not see on what grounds I can offer an opinion . . . Neither history nor pedantry can set the norm.'

The authors of bestselling handbooks such as *Don't: A Manual of Mistakes and Improprieties More or Less Prevalent in Conduct and Speech* (1884) and *Poor Letter H: Its Use and Abuse* (1859) were not so reluctant to issue prescriptions as to what was acceptable and what was not. The extract from the former (see Box 6) demonstrates the close association between correct speech and good breeding, and the assumption that linguistic solecisms were indicative of vulgarity.

The regional variants tolerated in Ellis' definition of RP were subsequently reduced under the influence of the English boarding schools, which had a homogenizing effect on the standard accent. The importance of this factor was

---

BOX 6 *Extract from* Don't: A Manual of Mistakes and Improprieties More or Less Prevalent in Conduct and Speech *(1884)*

DON'T speak ungrammatically. Study books of grammar, and the writings of the best authors.

DON'T pronounce incorrectly. Listen to the conversation of cultivated people, and, if in doubt, consult the dictionaries.

DON'T call your servants *girls*. Call the cook *cook*, and the nurse *nurse*, and the housemaids *maids*.

DON'T use slang. There is some slang that, according to Thackeray, is gentleman slang, and other slang that is vulgar. If one does not know the difference, let him avoid slang altogether, and then he will be safe.

DON'T fall into the habit of repeating worn-out proverbs and overused quotations. It becomes not a little irritating to have to listen to one who ceaselessly applies or misapplies a threadbare stock of 'wise saws' and stupid sayings.

DON'T notice in others a slip in grammar or a mispronunciation in a way to cause a blush or to offend. If you refer to anything of the kind, do it courteously, and not in the hearing of other persons.

---

recognized by a later phonetician, Daniel Jones, who initially employed the term 'Public School Pronunciation' for the standard adopted in his *English Pronouncing Dictionary* (1917), and reverted to Received Pronunciation in a later edition of 1926.

While Jones' early work was characterized by a disinterested approach to a standard of speech, he subsequently came to view the establishment of such a standard as a prerequisite for a civilized society: 'You cannot produce a uniform high standard of social life in a community without producing a uniform high standard of speech.' By this time, RP was established as a class accent: a form of speech which was not regionally inflected and which was associated exclusively with the upper classes.

The establishment of RP as a standard of pronunciation was further encouraged by the requirement that it be used by announcers employed by the British Broadcasting Corporation (BBC), when the organization was founded in the 1920s. To ensure that standards of speech were maintained, Lord Reith established the Committee on Spoken English, whose role was to adjudicate between alternative pronunciations, and which, in 1929, published a list of *Recommendations for Pronouncing Doubtful Words*. While many of the recommendations it issued remain relevant today, including the requirement that initial 'h' is sounded in *hotel* and *humour*, others, such as the pronunciation of *housewifery* as 'huzzifry' and *forehead* as 'forred' have changed under the influence of their spelling. In the case of *garage*, the guide's initial recommendation, 'garraazh', was changed to 'garridge' in a revised edition of 1931.

Although the committee was disbanded in 1939, the policy that all announcers must be RP speakers was only overturned in the 1960s. There was a relaxation of this stricture during the Second World War when Yorkshire-born Wilfred Pickles was employed as a newsreader. But this was not a move designed to challenge the hegemony of RP or to promote regional inclusivity; it was instead driven by the belief that the Germans would not be able to understand or imitate Pickles' Yorkshire brogue. The experiment was soon abandoned under pressure from listeners, who claimed to find it impossible to believe news read in such tones. As late as the 1980s, Scottish newsreader Susan Rae found herself dropped by the BBC following complaints from the public about falling standards of pronunciation. She was not reinstated until the early 2000s.

RP retains its status as a prestigious form of spoken English today, even though it is only employed by around 5 per cent of the population of Britain; its social cachet, however, is only recognized in certain social groups. In the opinion poll quoted earlier, it was predominantly an older group who expressed a preference for RP; younger people viewed RP speakers as cold, aloof, and snobbish. It is in recognition of this perception that some British politicians today tone down their RP accents when addressing diverse groups of blue-collar workers; and since this generally involves adopting features of the Cockney accent, this variety is known humorously as 'Mockney'.

This mixing of RP and Cockney features lies behind the emergence of a genuine south-eastern variety known as Estuary English. First appearing in the 1980s, Estuary English has its origins in the counties around the Thames estuary, but is now spreading throughout the south-east. It is characterized by a number of Cockney features such as 'glottaling', the replacement of 't' with a glottal stop in words like *bottle*; 'l-vocalization', in which 'l' is replaced by a vowel, found in the pronunciation of *milk* as 'miouk'; and 'th-fronting', in which 'th' is replaced by 'f': 'fink' and 'fing' instead of 'think' and 'thing'.

Because these features are traditionally socially stigmatized, the spread of Estuary English is typically reported as evidence of social decline by the British media. In 1999, the *Daily Telegraph* cricket correspondent, Michael Henderson, attacked the newly appointed English captain Nasser Hussain's glottal stops, claiming that 'Somebody who went to a good university has no excuse for speaking in that ghastly estuary sludge. Verbal imprecision often reveals mental laziness. Be a good chap, skipper, use the letter T. It's not there just to keep S and U company.'

There are a number of misconceptions in this attack, the most fundamental of which is the idea that pronunciation should follow spelling, and that failing to sound a particular letter is evidence of laziness; but in fact, the glottal stop requires greater physical exertion than the 't' sound does. But this rant has nothing to do with the linguistics of speech and writing; it is rather the expression of a deep-rooted social prejudice that demands that the English cricket captain, an alumnus of Durham university, should speak with an RP, rather than an Estuary, accent.

Good Grammar

For many people today the term *grammar* signifies a set of prescriptions governing correct usage: do not split an infinitive, avoid double negatives, never begin a sentence with a conjunction nor end it with a preposition. But for linguists, grammar refers to the set of rules by which words are organized into meaningful units.

An understanding of grammar is a crucial step in the development of a sophisticated handling of English; yet, for many people the teaching of grammar was handled in an atomistic manner: pupils were taught to identify parts of speech—nouns, verbs, adjectives—for no clear purpose. But, while learning how to identify parts of speech may have few benefits in itself, gaining insights into English grammar is an important step towards a deeper and more sophisticated understanding of how English works, and how to employ it effectively.

When discussing the value of a grasp of grammar, it is important to distinguish between covert and overt knowledge. All native speakers acquire a covert knowledge of English from the language spoken around them. As early as the age of two, children have acquired the rule that most English verbs form their past tense by adding an 'ed' suffix, enabling them to form past tenses of verbs without having heard them before. By hearing *I walked*, a two-year-old child is capable of extrapolating that the correct past tense of *talk* is *talked*. We know that children acquire the rule, rather than simply repeat forms they have heard, because they tend to overgeneralize and produce incorrect forms, such as *I singed* and *I goed*.

An overt knowledge of grammar—that is, a conscious understanding of the grammatical rules that underpin such constructions—must be learned through special study. That such knowledge is not innate becomes clear when you ask a native speaker of English to explain some point of grammar, such as why the past tense of *walk* is *walked*, whereas the past tense of *go* is *went*.

If we compare this kind of grammatical rule with ones like 'do not split an infinitive', there is a clear distinction; where rules for forming past tenses cannot be broken, the latter kind of rule can be, and frequently is, flouted. While there are no situations in which the phrase 'I goed to school' is acceptable, it is quite common to come across a sentence like 'Don't forget to quickly call Mum.' In fact, most people would naturally choose this construction rather than a more awkward, and more ambiguous, alternative like 'Don't forget quickly to call Mum.' (Does the *quickly* refer to the calling or the forgetting?) This comparison shows that, where the first type of rule is a genuine grammatical requirement, the second is a stylistic preference, which has no bearing upon the real structure of the language.

Even without any formal grammatical training, native English speakers acquire vast numbers of complex rules. Take the following two sentences. Which is correct?

The little yellow book.
The yellow little book.

All speakers of English are able to agree that the first is the correct version without any difficulty. But few can explain why this is correct, or why the alternative is unacceptable. In cases like this we intuit that certain constructions are impossible because they 'sound wrong' (recall Mark Forsyth's SWANS test in Chapter 3), but find it very hard to formulate what rules they contravene.

The reason why 'The little yellow book' is correct is that English has a rule that adjectives referring to size precede colour adjectives. This is not a rule we are taught in school, nor are many people aware of it. It is a rule we internalize as a child by listening to adult speech and extrapolating from it. If children can learn English grammar without realizing it, you might be wondering why we should waste classroom time teaching it to them. One reason is that, while this method of internalizing grammatical structures works well for young children, it becomes considerably harder as we get older. Furthermore, there is an added interest in knowing why a language works in the way it does: understanding such rules enables a more sophisticated awareness of when it is acceptable to deviate from them, and what kinds of deviation are permissible.

It was gaining an understanding of precisely this rule that kindled the philological interests of the young J. R. R. Tolkien. Having been informed by his mother that he could not begin his story with 'a green great dragon', the seven-year-old Tolkien was prompted to begin a lifetime's pondering on the structure of languages. Recounting the episode in a letter to W. H. Auden in 1955, the sixty-three-year-old Tolkien, now Professor of English Language at Oxford University, added: 'I wondered why and I still do.'

The earliest grammatical descriptions of English appeared in the sixteenth century, although many of these were written in Latin. Given that grammatical instruction prior to this had focused on the Latin language, it is not surprising that these early grammarians based their grammars of English on the model of Latin. The title of John Hewes' work of 1624 neatly summarizes its agenda in making English grammar conform to that of Latin: *A Perfect Survey of The English Tongve, Taken According to the Vse and Analogie of the Latine.* Since English is not derived from Latin, this is not a helpful model. Despite this, eighteenth-century grammarians persisted in imposing the Latinate model on English, as exemplified by this treatment of the English noun declension by Wells Egelsham in his *A Short Sketch of English Grammar* (1780):

	Singular	Plural
Nominative	a lord	lords
Genitive	of a lord, or, a lord's	of lords
Dative	to a lord	to lords
Accusative	a lord	lords
Vocative	o lord	o lords
Ablative	by, from, of, and with a lord	lords

Where Latin nouns have different endings for these various cases, English makes almost no distinction between the nominative, accusative, dative, vocative, and ablative cases in this paradigm.

Not all grammarians of this period were in thrall to the model of Latin; American linguist and lexicographer Noah Webster (1758–1843) dismissed the contention that the only way of truly grasping English grammar was by first learning Latin grammar as 'a stupid opinion' (see Box 7 for the full quotation).

Despite such enlightened opinions, the Latinate model was to survive into the twentieth century in the English classroom. One grammar used in English secondary schools in the opening years of the twentieth century includes exercises in which pupils are required to parse, or diagram, sentences, identifying whether a noun is in the nominative or objective case. *Gwynne's Grammar* (2013) continues this tradition; it is shot through with references to Latin grammar and draws extensively on its terminology.

BOX 7 *Noah Webster, Preface to* A Grammatical Institute of the English Language *(1784)*

'We are apt to be surprised, that men who made the languages their principal study, and during their whole lives were employed in teaching youth, should not discover that the Grammar of one language would not answer for another; but our wonder will cease when we reflect, that the English nation at large have, till very lately, entertained the idea that our language was incapable of being reduced to a system of rules; and that even now many men of much classical learning warmly contend that the only way of acquiring, a grammatical knowledge of the English Tongue, is first to learn a Latin Grammar. That such a stupid opinion should ever have prevailed in the English nation—that it should still have advocates—nay that it should still be carried into practice, can be resolved into no cause but the amazing influence of habit upon the human mind.'

An understanding of arcane terms of Latin grammar continues to hold social capital today. In his *Proposals for Perfecting the English Language* (1742), Thomas Cooke lamented that English cannot hope to imitate the excellence of Latin with its gerunds; despite being of very minor importance for an understanding of English grammar, knowing how to identify gerunds and gerundives continues to function as the hallmark of a sound grammatical education. The twelfth and final question of a 'good grammar' quiz published in *The Telegraph* newspaper in 2013 asked its readers to identify 'Which of these names is in fact the nominative feminine singular of the gerundive mood imported direct from Latin?' (In case your memory of gerundives is hazy, the answers are *Amanda* and *Miranda*.)

The earliest grammar books were comparatively descriptive in their approach, recording alternative constructions in recognition of the way speakers may vary an utterance depending on factors such as register, formality, and context. Although they tended to ignore dialectal differences, these grammarians did not censure variation within the emerging standard, or 'general', dialect. William Bullokar's *Pamphlet for English Grammar* (1586), for example, the first such book to be written in English, includes alternative forms of the verb *to be*, *ar* and *be*, third-person singular present-tense endings, *hath* and *has*, and second-person plural pronouns, *ye* and *you*. But this descriptive tolerance soon gave way to an increasingly prescriptive agenda. While some eighteenth-century grammarians recognized that alternative constructions rarely conveyed precisely the same meaning, most subscribed to the 'doctrine of correctness', which insisted that every construction was either right or wrong, 'barbarous', 'vulgar', or 'improper'.

Robert Lowth, whose *A Short Introduction to English Grammar* (1762) was especially influential, established the principle that a grammar should be based upon rules rather than on custom and usage, since even the greatest authors were guilty of committing errors. This has given rise to the tendency today to judge all forms of English according to the standard of formal written English. But, since the formal and informal modes are distinct, with their own set of functions, different grammatical conventions apply. Even this dichotomy is too crude, however, since it ignores the considerable amount of stylistic variation that is possible along the continuum that separates informal from more formal types of discourse.

To demonstrate the importance of distinguishing between speech and writing for our understanding of Standard English grammar, consider the following example. Imagine answering the telephone and receiving the following three replies:

Who's that?
Who am I speaking to?
To whom am I speaking?

What different assumptions would you make about the speaker at the other end of the line in each case? All three options are acceptable within Standard English, but each represents a different level of formality. The second is probably the most natural response in such a context. The first example comes across as brusque, suggesting impatience and a lack of concern for the niceties of polite discourse. By contrast, the third example is very formal, employing a construction now usually restricted entirely to the written language.

If we judge these sentences by the rules of Standard English grammar, based upon the formal written mode, the third sentence is correct. This is because *whom* is the accusative form of the pronoun *who*, required here after the preposition *to*. But this would be to insist upon a very forced and artificial mode of speech that would seem overly formal and pretentious in most interactions. To paraphrase American journalist Calvin Trillin, the result would be to make everyone sound like a butler.

The replacement of the accusative pronoun *whom* with the nominative form *who* has been underway since the fifteenth century; it is particularly common in questions of this kind, where the pronoun has been 'fronted'—shifted to the beginning of the sentence. Because this position is typically occupied by the subject in English, speakers often substitute the *who* pronoun in such positions, especially in speech.

So what is the future for *whom*? Will it be replaced by *who*, or does it continue to play a useful role? Despite the provocative title of his book, *For Who the Bell Tolls*, *Guardian* style guru David Marsh argues that learning to distinguish between *who* and *whom* remains desirable. But the reason he offers has nothing to do with grammatical or semantic clarity; it is driven by a concern to avoid embarrassing howlers. Having quoted a string of supposedly great writers who commit this egregious error, Marsh concludes: 'The main reason you need to know the difference, however, is so you don't make the mistake of using *whom* when it should be *who*.' This is a classic instance of the doctrine of correctness in the tradition of *Don't: A Manual of Mistakes and Improprieties*; but such advice is inherently self-defeating. Why would anyone run the risk of using *whom* when getting it wrong invites intellectual and social ridicule?

This example shows that, despite the popular view that learning grammar is concerned with negotiating a tightrope of rights and wrongs, Standard English encompasses a range of alternative constructions from which users select according to factors such as the medium, the context, register, level of formality, and so on. To insist that there is one and only one correct version in all contexts is to reduce the language's flexibility and communicative and pragmatic functions needlessly. In Chapters 5 and 6 we will pursue this idea further, investigating a number of different varieties of English as evidence of the richness of the language, its range of forms, and its functions.

5

Varieties

Dialects

Although the word *dialect* is loosely synonymous with a regional form of language, the word technically refers to any specific kind of language, reflecting its origins in the Greek word *dialektos* 'manner of speaking'. A regional dialect refers to the language spoken in a particular part of a country, while a social dialect, or *sociolect*, is the language used by a social group, such as the Standard English we examined in Chapter 4. In this first section we will investigate how language varies according to region, and in a subsequent section we will consider language variation according to use.

Although the concept of the regional dialect is well established, it is surprisingly hard to pin down. We can talk about the dialect of a large British county such as Devon, but can there really be said to be just one such dialect? A large area such as Devon might well comprise several dialects, but how many, and where do the boundaries lie? While there may be clear differences between the dialect of Devon and those of neighbouring south-western counties like Dorset and Somerset, these need not necessarily map neatly onto county boundaries. If you were to travel between Devon and Dorset you might notice shifts in linguistic usage, but these are minor and frequently imperceptible distinctions. This gradual shading of dialects is known to scholars as the 'dialect continuum'.

Similar problems arise when we try to define the difference between *dialect* and *language*. Superficially, this seems a more straightforward distinction, since we can define German as the language spoken in Germany, Dutch as the language of the Netherlands, and so on. A language is sometimes defined as a dialect with a flag; an axiom that helps to remind us that such distinctions are sociopolitical rather than linguistic.

German and Dutch are historically related languages, deriving from a single ancestor known as West Germanic (from which English also derives). Travelling across the boundary separating the two countries may necessitate a change in the official title of the language, but in reality the dialects spoken on the borders are remarkably similar. In the case of languages like Danish and Norwegian, the two languages are sufficiently similar to be mutually comprehensible, as are, to a lesser extent, Danish and Swedish.

Similar issues complicate our definition of the English language, especially now that it is spoken in so many different countries. Are American English and British English sufficiently distinct to be considered different languages, or are they both types of English? This is a question that we will consider in Chapter 6. What about the distinction between varieties spoken in Britain? The case of Scots and English offers a particularly vexed example.

Scots

Scots is one of several languages spoken in Scotland today. Although it has much in common with English, it differs in important ways from both Standard English and Scottish Standard English (essentially Standard English spoken with a Scottish accent). The similarities between English and Scots are the result of their historical ties; Scots is derived from the Northumbrian dialect of Old English, used in the area between the rivers Humber and Forth. As the kingdom of Scotland became separated from northern England, so its dialect diverged from that spoken south of the border; this variety came to be known as *Scottis*, rather than the earlier *Inglis*.

Many of the major linguistic differences between Scots and English can be traced back to the Older Scots period (1100–1700). Where the long 'aa' sound in Old English words like *stan*, *ham* (*stone*, *home*) came to be pronounced with lip-rounding in southern dialects of Middle English (*stoon*, *hoom*), Scots preserved the 'aa' sound; this has given rise to Modern Scots *stane* and *hame*. The Middle English long 'oo' sound in *foot* was pronounced further towards the front of the mouth in Older Scots; this is the source of Modern Scots *fuit* 'foot' and *guid* 'good'.

Older Scots dialects were only partially affected by the Great Vowel Shift that revolutionized English pronunciation in the sixteenth century (see Chapter 2). Where English accents replaced the long 'uu' vowel in words like *house* with a diphthong (the two separate vowel sounds heard in the southern English pronunciation of *house*), this change did not happen in Scots. Consequently, modern Scots dialects have preserved the Middle English 'uu' in words like *how* and *now*; think of the Scots cartoon *The Broons* (The Browns).

Differences in the pronunciation of consonants between Scots and Standard English include the preservation of the Middle English 'hw' sound in words like *which*, *when*, and *what*—a sound that was dropped in most English accents in the fifteenth century, although it was preserved in Standard English spelling.

Although pronunciation is the most obvious area of difference, there are many variations between Scots and Standard English grammar and lexicon. Grammatical discrepancies include verb constructions: 'Your hair needs washed', where Standard English would say 'needs washing'; alternative pronouns: *yous* 'you plural', *thir* 'these', *thae* 'those', and syntactic constructions like 'the back of 6', referring to a short time after 6 o'clock.

Differences in vocabulary include the use of words only found in Scots, such as *wee* 'small', *dreich* 'dreary', *fearty* 'coward', *glaikit* 'stupid', and *oxter* 'armpit', often the result of borrowing from other languages, such as Gaelic, Norwegian, and French. A number of words closely associated with Scottish culture derived from Gaelic have now entered Standard English; these include *claymore* (Gaelic *claidheamh mòr* 'great sword') and *whisky* (Gaelic *uisge beatha* 'water of life').

Despite the rich literary and linguistic legacy of Older Scots, the role of Scots changed substantially following the ascendancy of James VI of Scotland to the English throne as

James I in 1603, and the union of the parliaments in 1707. Unification led to the replacement of Scots with English; when a vernacular Bible came to replace the Latin Vulgate in Scotland, it was the Authorized Version—dedicated to the Scottish King James—which was adopted, rather than a translation into Scots. As a consequence, the prestige varieties in Scotland today are Standard English and Scottish Standard English, although Scots continues to be spoken widely and retains considerable cultural capital among Scottish nationalists.

Like English and other independent languages, Scots comprises several distinct dialects: Insular (the dialects of Orkney and Shetland), Northern (including the Doric—spoken in Aberdeen and the north-east), Central, and Southern (spoken in the Borders). Scots has its own tradition of codification, beginning with John Jamieson's *An Etymological Dictionary of the Scottish Language* (1808). Jamieson's dictionary is the earliest instance of an attempt to codify a non-standard version of English (although a manuscript containing an earlier incomplete and unpublished Scottish dictionary by Dr Johnson's biographer James Boswell has recently been discovered); however, Jamieson's text and definitions are in Standard English.

The twelve-volume *Dictionary of the Older Scottish Tongue* (covering the period from the twelfth to the end of the seventeenth centuries) and the ten-volume *Scottish National Dictionary* (comprising material from the eighteenth century to the present day), now merged electronically as the *Dictionary of the Scots Language*, provide the Scots language and its speakers with parallel resources for studying the history of Scots as the *OED* does for the English language. Despite these resources, no standard variety of Scots exists today; a twentieth-century attempt to produce an artificial standard written form, known as *Lallans*, has not won widespread support.

Is Scots a dialect of English, or a language in its own right? The linguistic evidence points both ways. At some places on the dialect continuum, English and Scots are mutually comprehensible, while at others (the insular and Doric dialects for example) they are linguistically further apart. But, ultimately, the answer depends more on political orientation than linguistic factors. The comparison with the relationships between Dutch and German, Danish and Norwegian—distinct languages with considerable linguistic similarities—with which we began seems a particularly useful parallel in the case of Scots and English. Scots speakers seeking the independence of the Scottish nation are likely to view Scots as a separate language, while those in favour of preserving the union will be content to view their language as closely affiliated to English.

Attitudes

Despite their status as local varieties, Modern English dialects are frequently viewed today as socially inferior to Standard English. This stigmatization of regional varieties is a relatively recent phenomenon; it is the result of social prejudice rather than linguistic factors. As I stressed in Chapter 4, since variation is the natural state of a language, we would expect differences to arise in forms of English spoken in locations that are geographically separate.

If we go back to the earliest examples of English, there is clear evidence for at least four dialects of Old English: West Saxon (associated with the kingdom of Wessex), Kentish, Mercian (used in the Midlands), and Northumbrian (used north of the river Humber). Because there was no single standard variety of Middle English we find huge variation in the written records from this period; since dialect variation was so prevalent, no one variety was considered superior to another.

It is in the fifteenth and sixteenth centuries that we witness the beginnings of dialect prejudice; an early instance can be traced in the writings of a chronicler named John Trevisa, who complained that the Northumbrian dialect was so 'scharp, slitting [biting] and frottynge [grating] and unshape [unshapely]' that southerners like himself were unable to understand it. In the early seventeenth century, Alexander Gill, writing in Latin, labelled 'Occidentalium' (or Western dialect) the 'greatest barbarity' and claimed that the English spoken by a Somerset farmer could easily be mistaken for a foreign language.

Despite such remarks, the social stigmatization of dialect was not fully articulated before the eighteenth century, when a provincial accent became a badge of social and intellectual inferiority. In his *Tour Thro' the Whole Island of Great Britain* (1724–27), Daniel Defoe reported his encounter with the 'boorish country speech' of Devon—known to the locals as *jouring*—which was barely comprehensible to outsiders. Having heard a schoolboy read the following lesson from Scripture: 'Chav a doffed me cooat, how shall I don't, chav a wash'd my veet, how shall I moil'em?' (Song of Solomon 5:3), Defoe records his astonishment at finding that the 'dexterous dunce' was reading from a copy of the Bible in which the words and spelling were those of the standard text: 'I have put off my coat, how shall I put it on, I have wash'd my feet, how shall I defile them?' In this brief anecdote we witness many of the same assumptions and prejudices that are associated with dialect speech in England today.

Accents

Although the two are often used loosely as synonyms, there is a technical distinction between a dialect and an accent. Where accent refers exclusively to pronunciation, dialect includes accent, grammar, and vocabulary. All speakers of English use an accent; despite this, it is common to hear RP speakers described as having no accent. This view is probably influenced by the idea of RP as a standard by which other accents are measured, and its status as a variety that is not regionally delineated.

Although the various accents of English differ in numerous complex ways, the following sentence was proposed by linguist Peter Trudgill as containing the major diagnostic features which enable speakers of different dialects to be distinguished: Very few cars made it up the long hill. Included here are such important distinguishing criteria as whether the speaker uses the southern 'up' or the northern 'oop', drops the initial 'h' in *hill*, and the 'r' in *car*. The geographical distribution of these features can be partly explained by reference to linguistic history, as we can see from the distribution of rhotic accents (those which pronounce 'r' after vowels) and non-rhotic accents (which do not pronounce 'r' in such positions) today.

As Modern English spelling implies, the rhotic pronunciation was a feature of the London accent when spelling was standardized in the fifteenth century. Spelling evidence shows that the non-rhotic pronunciation first appeared in East Anglia, spreading to the capital in the sixteenth century. It was not until the nineteenth century that the non-rhotic pronunciation was fully accepted into prestigious speech; the poet John Keats (1795–1821) was criticized by reviewers for relying on 'Cockney rhymes' such as *thorns/fawns*.

While the dropping of 'r' had spread to most other accents of England by the eighteenth century, rhoticity remains a feature of accents spoken in the geographically more extreme areas of England today: the south-west, north-west, and north-east. This distribution suggests that the loss of this feature has been spreading outwards from the eastern dialects since the fifteenth century, but has not yet affected these few remaining strongholds. From this development we might predict that postvocalic 'r' will at some stage be entirely lost from accents of English, though it is impossible to determine exactly when this process will reach completion.

Dialect Grammars

Where regional accents can evoke positive associations—attractive, friendly, trustworthy—regional grammars are almost always viewed negatively. While accents are usually considered solely according to place, discussions of dialect grammars frequently confuse regional and social factors. Double negatives, for example, have now become so wide-spread that they are viewed simply as non-standard, or wrong. But recent dialect research has shown that double negatives are considerably less common in northern dialects, indicating that this is a regional phenomenon.

Another frequent mistake is to confuse non-standard dialects with informal usage. But it is perfectly possible to speak informally using Standard English, just as it is possible to adopt a formal register using a regional dialect. Compare the following two sentences:

You are making me bloody cross.
You is making me extremely irate.

The first is written with Standard English grammar, but using informal vocabulary, including the taboo word *bloody*. The second sentence employs the non-standard verb construction *is making*; the word choice, however, indicates a more formal register.

In practice it would be very unusual to hear a non-standard variety spoken in a formal context. What would your response be to hearing the following observation on the BBC weather forecast: 'I'm stood outside the BBC weather centre. The weather is somewhat inclement but there ain't no sign of precipitation'? The word choice indicates the expected formal register, even though the sentence uses non-standard grammatical features. There is no linguistic reason why this should sound so odd to our ears; the disjunction is a purely social phenomenon, caused by our being accustomed to associating formal language with Standard English. This becomes all the more apparent when we consider other countries, such as Norway and Switzerland, where it would be perfectly possible to hear dialect speech in such formal contexts.

Although they are dismissed as linguistically inferior versions of Standard English, dialect grammars are frequently the result of changes that have been artificially halted by the fixed forms of Standard English. For instance, there is a tendency for dialects to use a simplified version of the present-tense verb conjugation found in Standard English. Standard English has the following forms:

I take
You (sg.) take
He/She/It takes
We take
You (pl.) take
They take

This is a reduced form of the verb conjugation found in earlier stages of English, which attested a richer set of endings. As a comparison, here is the equivalent conjugation for this verb in Middle English (*c.*1500):

I take
Thou takest
He/She/It taketh
We taken
Ye taken
They taken

In Standard English the 'est' and 'en' endings were reduced to 'e', and a northern dialect 's' replaced the southern 'eth' ending in the third-person singular. This is a change that was completed by the early seventeenth century; it can be observed in progress during Shakespeare's lifetime: his early plays show greater use of 'eth' than his later works.

Although the standard Modern English paradigm lacks most of the distinctive endings found in earlier varieties, even the 's' ending itself is somewhat redundant, since the same information can be gleaned from the subject. Modern dialects of English have ironed out such redundancies, creating an even more simplified paradigm:

I takes
You takes
He/She/It takes
We takes
You takes
They takes

An alternative simplification, in which the 's' ending is omitted, so that all persons of the verb are endingless, is found in a number of English dialects, such as that of Norwich, and of American English, including Chicano English (a form of English influenced by Spanish, discussed further in Chapter 6) and African American English.

The replacement of the second person plural pronoun *ye* with Modern English *you* is part of a larger process that witnessed a reduction in the number of pronoun forms that accompanied the levelling of inflexional endings. The *you* pronoun is historically the object (accusative) form; as the system of case-marking was replaced by one relying upon more fixed word order, fewer distinct pronoun forms were required. This triggered a merger of the formerly distinct accusative (direct object) and dative (indirect object) pronouns. In the spoken language, this merger even affected the subject pronoun, eventually leading to the complete replacement of *ye* by *you*.

The tendency to replace the subject with the object pronoun remains common in spoken English today, although it is condemned by purists who vehemently oppose constructions such as: 'Me and Billy are going to the shops'. Despite the strong opposition, this is evidently a natural tendency which can be traced back to the Early Modern period, and which might well have resulted in the replacement of *I* with *me* if it had not been artificially halted by eighteenth-century prescriptivism.

Not all distinctions between standard and non-standard varieties are simplifications. An important difference between the Middle and Modern English pronoun systems is the loss of the singular/plural distinction triggered by the dropping of the second-person pronoun *thou*. This has left a gap in the Standard English pronoun system, making it impossible to distinguish between you (singular) and you (plural); many dialects, however, have developed alternative plural pronouns, such as *yous*, *yez*, and *y'all*, which enable such a distinction; in some northern varieties of Modern English the problem was avoided by the retention of the *thou* pronoun. Such innovations serve as a useful corrective to the claim that dialect grammars are necessarily simplifications and corruptions of the linguistically superior Standard English.

Dialect Vocabulary

Where dialect grammars generally have negative social connotations, regional vocabulary is often viewed with affection and closely bound up with local identity. A large project conducted by the BBC, The Voices Project, aimed to collect local vocabulary from across the UK during 2004–05. The project was greeted with considerable enthusiasm, eliciting a wealth of variant terms and demonstrating the vibrancy and longevity of dialect vocabulary.

For just one of its chosen categories—words used to refer to the soft shoe worn by children for Physical Education—more than fifty different terms were submitted to the project's website (see Box 8). It is not just specific objects for which a rich collection of regional terms were reported; words for feeling cold included *nesh, shrammed, nobbling, foonert, chanking,* and *braw.*

BOX 8 *Dialect words collected by the BBC Voices Project*

child's soft shoes worn for Physical Education: *pumps, daps, plimsolls, gutties, sandshoes, gym shoes, plimmies, sneakers, sannies,* and *runners.*

play truant: *skive, bunk off, wag, skip, mitch, dog, hookey, twag, sag, nick off.*

lacking money: *skint, poor, hard up, brassick, penniless, short, boracic, potless, strapped, stoney.*

left-handed: *cack handed, lefty, left handed, southpaw, corrie fisted, caggy handed, sinister, caggy, left hooker, keg handed.*

Derogatory terms were also found to include a diverse regional lexicon; the words submitted to describe a 'young person in cheap trendy clothes and jewellery' reflected a rich range of insulting labels. The accompanying maps show that some of these, such as *chav*, are in widespread use, whereas others are associated with particular regional pockets. *Pikey* is most frequently used in London, *scally* is found most commonly in the north-west, and *charva* in the north-east, whereas *ned* is predominantly recorded in the west of Scotland.

The Future

While the BBC Voices project suggests that regional vocabulary is flourishing in Britain, it remains difficult to gauge how widely these words extend within their local communities and across the generations. Since we saw in Chapter 4 how Estuary English is spreading throughout the south-east and well beyond, we might wonder whether traditional rural dialects of English are disappearing.

The spread of Estuary English is not the only threat to regional usage; rural dialect distinctions are also being reduced via a process known as 'levelling': dialects which were formerly distinct are becoming more similar. Does this mean that dialect differences are being lost entirely, pointing to a future in which everyone will speak Standard English, or perhaps Estuary English?

Such a suggestion is not new; the stigmatization of dialect, combined with major social changes associated with the Industrial Revolution and urbanization, prompted a fear

113

among nineteenth-century philologists that regional dialects would be eradicated. In response to this, the English Dialect Society was founded by W. W. Skeat in 1873, launching the collection of materials that led to the publication of Joseph Wright's *English Dialect Dictionary* (1898–1905) and *English Dialect Grammar* (1905). In the preface to the *English Dialect Grammar*, Wright predicted that the dialects recorded in his work would fall out of use entirely within twenty years of its publication.

The next systematic attempt to collect dialect materials was launched in the 1940s by Harold Orton, a Professor of English at Leeds University. This survey conducted field-work in more than three hundred locations across England, collecting the language of older, working-class males in rural communities (so-called NORMs—Non-mobile Older Rural Males) in order to elicit the most conservative forms of speech. The informants were interviewed by researchers who recorded responses for some 1,300 linguistic items, relating to topics such as farming, housekeeping, animals, and nature. This project culminated in the publication of the collected materials in four volumes (1962–71), followed by *The Linguistic Atlas of England* (1978), which supplied maps indicating the geographical range of dialect words and pronunciations (see Figure 9). Advances in technology in the 1950s meant that recordings could be made of interviews with informants, and a selection of the original recordings are now available on the British Library's website.

For the project's instigator, Stanley Ellis, the undertaking was timely and urgent, since the traditional dialects were being lost as quickly as they could record them: 'Very often

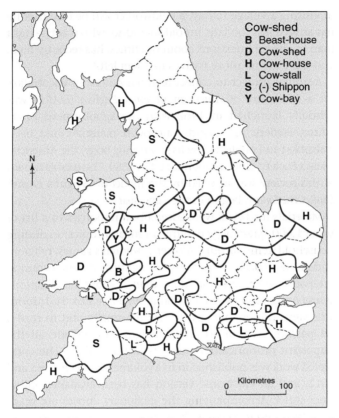

Figure 9 Dialect map: words used to refer to a cow-shed in England and Wales.

in visiting a village to-day, a fieldworker will be told that he has arrived just too late, for old so-and-so, who was the right man to answer questions about old times, has recently died, and there are no more natives like him left.'

A similar project to collect regional American vocabulary for a *Dictionary of American Regional English* (*DARE*) was officially launched in 1962 with the appointment of its editor, Frederic G. Cassidy, although materials had been assembled and published by its sponsoring body, the American Dialect Society, since its foundation in 1889. The establishment of this society was inspired by the model of Wright's *English Dialect Dictionary*, begun in the same year.

Materials for *DARE* were based upon responses to a list of some 1,600 questions covering a range of topics, including household items, farming, flowers, children's games, religion, and money, collected by a team of eighty fieldworkers during interviews conducted at more than a thousand locations across America between 1965 and 1970 (see Box 9). Informants were also encouraged to talk informally and to read a set passage, 'Arthur the Rat', designed to include all the important pronunciation variants in US English. The completed work was published in five volumes between 1985 and 2012, and an electronic version has been available online since 2013. Accompanying the dictionary entries are maps indicating where words were recorded, as well as supplementary information about the age, race, sex, education, and background of the informants.

Modern dialectology has made important departures from this methodology, with its focus on NORMs and reliance upon fixed questionnaires, in favour of analysing a broader

---

BOX 9 *Sample entries from the* Dictionary of American Regional English

....

feest: disgusted with, sated by, made nauseous by, nauseated.

honeyfuggle: to swindle or dupe, to intend to cheat or trick.

larruping: delicious, excellent.

mulligrubs: a condition of despondency or ill temper, a vague or imaginary unwellness.

rantum scoot: an outing with no definite destination.

toad-strangler: a very heavy rain.

yee-yaw: to swerve back and forth, wobble.

---

cross-section of the population and a larger selection of linguistic variables in a range of styles. Instead of focusing on the oldest members of established rural communities, modern studies have examined the speech of the geograph-ically and socially mobile, focusing particularly on the younger generation, who tend to be leaders of linguistic innovations. Rather than prompting informants to give one-word answers by asking questions of the type 'What do you call that?' in order to elicit words for abstruse farming terms such as the *stretcher*—the wooden rod that prevents the traces from chafing the leading horse in a team—modern dia-lectologists elicit data in a range of formats: reading a word list, reading a piece of text, and engaging in casual conversation.

The results of such studies have shown that, while these early dialectologists were undoubtedly right in noting the disappearance of some regional varieties, they were wrong to view this as the demise of regional speech. What was really happening was the replacement of older rural varieties with newer ones, often based in emerging urban centres.

Similar developments have been documented in new towns like Milton Keynes, established in the 1960s, where the first generation of children to have grown up there were found to have rejected the dialects used by their parents and those of the local Buckinghamshire area, in favour of a range of features typical of south-eastern dialects, including Cockney and Estuary English. Parallel studies in Reading and Hull have shown a similar process of dialect levelling reducing the differences between geographically distant varieties. In their place, new regional varieties are emerging and being spread over a wider geographical area, as more people move from inner cities to smaller suburban towns.

Working against this general levelling of local language is the association of dialect speech with identity and belonging. The role such values can play in reinforcing and preserving local language was identified by American sociolinguist William Labov in an investigation into the speech patterns of residents of Martha's Vineyard, an island off the coast of Massachusetts. Labov's research showed that a group of younger islanders had subconsciously adopted a pronunciation of words like *how* and *life* characteristic of a small community of local fisherman, setting them apart from the other residents. Since Martha's Vineyard is regularly overwhelmed by summer visitors from New England, whose presence is a bone of contention among local residents, Labov concluded that the adoption of these pronunciations by the young people was a deliberate attempt to identify with the local community rather than with the unwelcome tourists.

Registers

As well as varying according to the user, language also varies according to use—what is known as register variation. As users of English we instinctively recognize this fact when we adjust our language according to context; think of the way you would vary your language between talking to a child, giving a speech, writing a job application, and sending a text message to a close friend. Although we may not be able to explain the various linguistic modifications and accommodations involved, we consciously adapt our language to the situation. While many such switches are instinctive—speaking to a baby generally prompts the employment of a baby language known as 'motherese' (or, following a recognition that fathers speak to babies too, 'child-directed speech')—others are more artificial and must be explicitly taught, such as the conventions associated with formal letter-writing (whether, for example, to sign off 'yours sincerely' or 'yours faithfully').

There is, of course, considerable overlap between the linguistic features associated with various registers; it would be impossible to set out all the various registers available to a single speaker. To give a flavour of the language's flexibility and potential for creative engagement, the next section will investigate the emergence of new varieties associated with electronic communication.

Electronic Discourse

There has been much concern in the press about the linguistic poverty of this medium, and its corresponding corruption of the language as a whole. According to John Sutherland of University College London, writing in *The Guardian* in 2002, textspeak is 'bleak, bald, sad shorthand. Drab shrinktalk... Linguistically it's all pig's ear... it masks dyslexia, poor spelling and mental laziness. Texting is penmanship for illiterates.' In an article published in the *Daily Mail* in 2007, the broadcaster John Humphrys accused the texting generation of wrecking the English language, describing them as 'vandals who are doing to our language what Genghis Khan did to his neighbours eight hundred years ago.' But are such claims warranted? Let us start by considering the view that electronic communication is linguistically impoverished.

Neologisms

One of the distinctive features of electronic discourse is the coining of new words, characterized by clipped forms, such as *blog* (*weblog*) and *app* (*application*); blends, *blogosphere*, *twitterverse*; acronyms, *LOL* (laughing out loud), *TL;DR* (too long; didn't read); and fanciful respellings such as *phish* and *phreak*. In the case of words like *teh* and *pwn*, whose origins lie in the frequent mistyping of the correct forms *the* and *own*, it seems legitimate to wonder whether such demonstrably erroneous forms qualify as acceptable English words.

But, while the new formulations of electronic technology are often criticized for being ugly and illiterate, similar objections were raised when the word *television*, a blend of the Greek *telos* 'far' and the Latin *visio* 'see', was coined to refer to that new-fangled invention. For C. P. Scott, the word's mixed etymology heralded its doomed future: 'The word is half Greek, half Latin. No good can come of it.'

Such hybrid formations were denounced by H. W. Fowler in *Modern English Usage* (1926), although he conceded that the only way of identifying such 'barbarisms'— by consulting a competent philologist—would not always be practical. The objectionable examples cited by Fowler include *bureaucrat*, *cablegram*, and *electrocute*—none of which would be objected to today. As with many similar objections, one wonders whether Fowler's distaste was really directed at what the words represented, rather than the words themselves. Similarly, an antipathy for modern technology and the rapid social and cultural change it is precipitating drives many of the complaints directed at its linguistic content.

The rapid expansion and development of new technology and social media, combined with its inherently in-group, anti-authoritarian ethos, present particular challenges for those tasked with regulating usage. A recent attempt by the Académie Française to oblige the French Twitterati to use the term *mot-dièse* rather than the English *hashtag* to refer to the '#' symbol highlights the ineffectual nature of such pronouncements. Opponents of this ruling took to Twitter to ridicule this latest attempt to regulate online usage, employing the hashtag #fightingalosingbattle. Previous attempts by the Académie to outlaw the words *email* and *blog* proved similarly ineffective.

Despite the playful tendency that lies behind coinages associated with new technology, many such formations are created using more traditional methods. As a Germanic language, English has traditionally drawn upon affixes—grammatical units, known as 'morphemes', added to the beginnings (prefixes) and ends (suffixes) of words. Affixation was an especially productive means of expanding the lexicon in Old English, before the impact of French following the Norman Conquest, as it still is in other Germanic languages today (see Chapter 2).

In Old English the 'un' prefix was used as a negative marker, so that the opposite of *friþ* 'peace' was *unfriþ* 'war'; it was also added to verbs to indicate the reverse of an action, as in *unbindan* 'unbind'. Exactly the same process lies behind recent formations such as *unfollow* and *unfriend*—terms coined by the micro-blogging and social media platforms Twitter and Facebook. Although the majority of such uses cited in the *OED* are from the electronic realm, there is a single quotation from a seventeenth-century letter in which the writer expresses the hope that he and his recipient are not 'mutually Un-friended by this Difference which hath happened betwixt us.' Examples like this remind us that such formations are not new, nor are they restricted to electronic discourse.

The production of new words by blending two words together, creating what are known as 'portmanteau words', is not recent either. The term was invented by Lewis Carroll, or rather his creation Humpty Dumpty, who coined it when asked by Alice to explain the words *slithy* and *mimsy* in the poem *Jabberwocky*. He explains that these words are a blend of *lithe+slimy* and *flimsy+miserable*, and therefore function like a portmanteau suitcase, in which two distinct compartments are folded into one.

While these words have not stuck, Carroll's parallel coinage *chortle* (*chuckle+snort*) is still in use. Alongside such fanciful formations are everyday instances like *smog* (*smoke +fog*), *ginormous* (*gigantic+enormous*) and *Oxbridge* (*Oxford +Cambridge*). While blends are a characteristic feature of electronic discourse—think of *phablet*, *podcast*, *webinar*, *emoticon*—they are common in other areas, such as cookery— *brunch* and *cronut* (*croissant+doughnut*)—and entertainment— *docudrama* and *infomercial*.

Acronyms and initialisms (where the letters are pronounced separately) have similarly lengthy histories; even the contemporary-sounding *OMG* (Oh my God) has been traced back by the *OED* as far as 1917. The initialism *LOL* (Laughing out Loud) began life as a feature of electronic discourse; but its increasing use in speech as an acronym (pronounced as a single word 'lol') follows a similar path as *VAT*, and even *scuba* (Self-Contained Underwater Breathing Apparatus) and *radar* (Radio Detection and Ranging).

While electronic communication tends to favour abbreviations, the introduction of smartphones, with a full keyboard, and of unlimited texts, has tended to make logograms like *CU* 'see you', *L8R* 'later', and *H&* 'hand' less common in texting. While initialisms like *BTW* (by the way), *IMHO* (in my humble opinion), and *FWIW* (for what it's worth) can still be found, one suspects that some of those listed in texting manuals, such as *GD&R* (grinning ducking, and running), *FOTCL* (falling off the chair laughing), and *PMIJI* (please may I jump in), are more unusual.

Another common method of new word formation associated with electronic discourse is conversion, popularly known as 'verbing', by which a word shifts its class without any change in form. Examples of this include *Google it*, 'look it up using the search engine Google', *Facebook me* 'send me a message on Facebook', and *trend* 'be the subject of numerous posts on a social network site'. The Calvin and Hobbes cartoon from 1993 (Figure 10) shows that the idea that verbing 'weirds' language is not new; conversions of this kind, such as *action*, *dialogue*, *impact*, *interface*, are frequently cited in support of the view that managerial jargon is corrupting English. While verbing is popularly seen as a modern fad, it is much older; many unremarkable verbs in common use today, such as *rain*, *bottle*, and *near*, are the result of conversion.

As well as coining new formations, technological developments have led to changes in the uses of established words. A mouse can no longer simply be defined as 'a little animal haunting houses and corn fields, destroyed by cats', as it was by Dr Johnson in 1755. Trolls are not just found lurking under bridges preying on unsuspecting billy goats, tweeting is not limited to birds, and surfing no longer requires a surfboard.

Punctuation

The different pragmatic requirements of electronic discourse have prompted the development of a series of new

Figure 10 Calvin and Hobbes on 'verbing'.

conventions for the use of punctuation marks. The excessive use of exclamation marks, known as *bangorrhea*, omission of full-stops, and the apparently random use of capital letters has led many language purists to condemn the illiteracy of electronic discourse, and to fear for the future of traditional punctuation. But, far from indicating an ignorant misuse of traditional punctuation, electronic discourse has repurposed these marks to convey specific semantic and pragmatic effects.

In a face-to-face spoken interaction, the speaker receives continual feedback from the audience and so can gauge the impact of an utterance and make adjustments accordingly. During a spoken conversation it is possible to employ extra-linguistic cues like facial expression, tone of voice, intonation, volume, and hand gestures to help convey the correct tone of a message.

Written language relies upon punctuation to carry such information; but, because the repertoire of marks is restricted and predefined, the degree of attitudinal information that can be conveyed this way is limited. Since the recipient of the message is not physically present, it is not possible for the writer to respond to an individual's reaction while writing. Where a spoken interaction is generally between a small group of people, a written communication could potentially be read by a much larger number of unknown people, over a longer period of time. Predicting and pre-empting the range of possible reactions of a written text, therefore, is impossible.

Where do email, texting, instant-messaging, and tweeting fit into this speech and writing dichotomy? Since they are conveyed using written symbols without a physically present interlocutor, electronic messages clearly belong with the written medium. But they differ from traditional epistolary forms in being generally brief and written at speed, omitting the politeness strategies of a conventional letter, and with little or no revision. Where an exchange using the postal service, or 'snail mail', takes place over a period of days, an email interaction can happen in real time. It is this blending of features of speech and writing that has prompted David Crystal to characterize texting as 'speaking with your fingers'.

What appears to be a random and ignorant misapplication of the standard repertoire of punctuation marks in electronic discourse is, on closer examination, more often a sophisticated attempt to convey the attitudinal and emotional information typically associated with speech in a written medium. The standard range of punctuation marks allows questions and exclamations to be distinguished from statements, but it is not possible to indicate questions that are also exclamations. The interrobang, devised in 1962 by Martin K. Speckter, the head of an American advertising agency, was an attempt to fill this gap; in electronic communication it is common to find sentences ending with both a question mark and an exclamation mark: 'What were you thinking?!'

The exclamation mark has experienced something of a resurgence in the electronic age. F. Scott Fitzgerald considered their use the equivalent of laughing at one's own jokes, while H. W. Fowler viewed excessive use of the exclamation mark the sign of an amateur writer, or one attempting to add 'a spurious dash of sensation to something unsensational'. But the widespread use of exclamation marks in electronic discourse is not simply evidence of a modern delight in one's own humour, or a tendency to oversensationalize. Research has shown that they carry a range of exclamatory functions, including apologizing, challenging, thanking, agreeing, and showing solidarity. Attempts to defuse an argument, or to make a direct apology, are often strengthened by the use of exclamation marks: Calm down! My apologies!

Another method of conveying tone is to add an emoticon, or smiley. Early instances comprise ingenious attempts to use combinations of keyboard strokes to produce a facial expression as a means of conveying the speaker's mood, from the basic :-) to more complex and ambiguous examples, such as >:\ (supposedly intended to represent scepticism), and ;((which implies sadness with a hint of sarcasm). In general, the range of expressions is rather crude, and remains open to misinterpretation; does a smiling face indicate that you are laughing with someone or at them? Does the double smiley mouth mean you are very amused, or implying your recipient has a double chin? :-))

The restrictions imposed by the use of ASCII characters in emoticons have been overcome by the newer emoji, a small digital pictogram used to convey emotion or simple concepts in electronic communication. From the Japanese e- 'picture' + moji 'character', emojis were first deployed by Japanese teenagers on their pagers in the 1990s, and there are now nearly 800 characters in use. Use of emojis has expanded such that it is common for entire messages to be conveyed using these symbols—enabling them to be understood by speakers of any language. A crowd-sourced project has successfully translated the entirety of Herman Melville's classic novel *Moby Dick* using emojis. The limitations of the linguistic format are immediately apparent, however: in *Emoji Dick* the novel's famous opening 'Call me Ishmael' is represented, somewhat cryptically, by a series of icons showing a telephone, a man with a moustache, a boat, a whale, and an OK sign.

While exclamation marks, smileys, and emojis offer methods of defusing situations and apologizing, what happens when you want to deliberatively provoke or insult someone? Here traditional punctuation offers little help, since there are no marks that explicitly indicate anger or aggression. In electronic discourse, however, the use of capitals has become an established means of shouting, or expressing hostility towards your addressee. To write an email entirely in upper-case is seen as an act of deliberate aggression; a New Zealand woman was dismissed from her job for sending emails exclusively in capitals, which were deemed to be the cause of disharmony in the office. The US Navy was forced to change its policy of requiring all communications to be in upper-case, since sailors accustomed to reading text messages and emails considered the default use of capitals as the equivalent of being constantly shouted at.

Far from being an impoverished medium, electronic communication is characterized by creativity and playfulness, spawning new words, and repurposing traditional conventions of spelling and punctuation. Since emails, tweets, and text messages are intended to be short missives written in haste, without requiring the proofreading and revision that are commonly applied to more formal writing, it is not surprising that they commonly include spelling, punctuation, and typographical errors. Since messages posted on Twitter are limited to 140 characters, it is to be expected that tweeters have resorted to abbreviated spellings and light punctuation.

To view such features as evidence of illiteracy is to make the same mistake as judging dialect speech according to the conventions of standard written English. While it remains inappropriate to adopt a similarly relaxed attitude towards spelling, punctuation, and grammar in formal written English, this is an accepted aspect of electronic discourse. Attempts to police electronic usage and to insist its users follow conventional rules seem doomed to failure.

6

Global Englishes

In his *Elementarie* of 1582, Richard Mulcaster, headmaster of the Merchant Tailors' school, commented on the English language's limited coverage: 'our English tung...is of small reatch, it stretcheth no further than this Iland of ours, naie not there ouer all'. This situation was shortly to change in a dramatic way. At the time Mulcaster was writing, the number of native English speakers is estimated to have been between five and seven million; by the early twenty-first century that number had increased to around 450 million. A major reason for this huge expansion in speakers was the colonization of America, which began shortly after Mulcaster's work was published.

English in America

The first step in the spread of English across the globe was the successful settlement at Chesapeake Bay, named Jamestown and Virginia by the colonists who settled there. A second settlement followed with the arrival of a group of Puritans on the *Mayflower*, establishing a colony in Plymouth, Massachusetts. As the process of migration continued throughout the seventeenth century, the discrete dialect boundaries that had existed in England were jumbled up, as settlers from disparate English counties found themselves close neighbours.

As a consequence, new dialects emerged, drawing features from each of the contributing dialects and thereby giving rise to many of the differences that set American English apart from its British ancestor today. The Quakers from the midland and northern English counties brought the flatter and more fronted 'a' sound in *last*; this contrasts with the longer, back vowel found today in southern English accents in words like *path* and *bath*—the result of an eighteenth-century development. Puritans from the south-west brought the 'r' sound after vowels, as in *hard*.

Although today American English is frequently caricatured as a corrupting influence upon the purer tongue spoken in England, many of its characteristic features reflect the preservation of seventeenth-century usages. Where Received Pronunciation dropped the 'r' in *car* (see Chapter 5), this sound has been preserved in most American accents; the main exception is the speech of Boston, which continued to be influenced by the fashionable London accent in the nineteenth century, and where the non-rhotic ('r'-less) pronunciation is seen as highly distinctive—as captured in the stereotype phrase 'I parked the car in Harvard Yard'.

Other older usages that have been preserved in American speech include the unrounded vowel sound in *not* (compare the similar sound implied by the Middle English spelling *nat*), an 'h'-less pronunciation of *herb* (Middle English *erbe*), *dove* as the past tense form of *dive*, and *gotten*, an alternative past participle of *got* used in Middle English (preserved in the archaic phrase *ill-gotten gains*). Words considered distinctively American today have their roots in earlier varieties of English, such as *fall* for *autumn*, and the phrase *I guess*, frequently attested in Middle English.

This tendency for colonial varieties to preserve archaic features of the parent language is well attested; it is known to linguists as 'colonial lag'—a problematic term which should not be taken to imply that the language is trying to play catch-up. Just as it is important to avoid seeing a colonial variety as a lazy child, we should also be wary of exaggerating the view of American English as a purer form of English, preserving direct links to the Early Modern period. This view is most clearly articulated in the mythical notion that there are people living in the Appalachian hills of North Carolina who continue to talk like Shakespeare.

As well as preserving earlier features of English, American English imported words from the languages of other European settlers—speakers of French, Spanish, Portuguese, German, and Dutch. As with all other colonial varieties, it also adopted words from the native languages with which it came into contact, especially those referring to local flora, fauna, and customs. From the native American languages are derived *raccoon*, *opossum* (literally 'white dog'), *moccasins*, *wigwam* ('their house'), and *powwow* (from a root meaning 'he who dreams').

Patterns of borrowing varied geographically; while many Yiddish loanwords, such as *klutz*, *chutzpah*, *maven*, and *mensch*, have now percolated into General American, these were first adopted in large urban areas like New York City. Territories supported by the slave trade show the earliest introduction of words of African origin; from the Bantu language come words for foods—*goober* 'peanut', *gumbo* 'okra', and beliefs—such as *zombie*, referring to a corpse revived by witchcraft. The importation of these native American and African loanwords conceals a darker history of conquest, subjugation, slavery, and near extinction; the spread of English in North America came at the expense of the native languages and their speakers.

In spelling, American English largely follows the British model, though there are some distinctive differences. These were established by American lexicographer and spelling-reformer Noah Webster (1758–1843) and encoded in his *An American Dictionary of the English Language* (1828)—part of a deliberate attempt to set American English apart from its colonial ancestor. These spelling reforms were also designed to make American spelling reflect pronunciation more closely, hence the removal of the silent 'u' in *color, honor, favor*, and the use of 'er' instead of 're' in *meter* and *theater*. Not all of Webster's proposed changes caught on; reformed spellings such as *determin* 'determine', *altho* 'although', *crum* 'crumb', *ile* 'isle', *soop* 'soup', and *fashon* 'fashion' were a step too far.

But, while Webster was determined to assert the validity of a distinctively American language, drawing his evidence of usage from distinguished writers such as Franklin, Washington, and Adams, the view that Americans spoke a corrupted form of English (a 'pye-bald' dialect in the words of one writer) was already prevalent among citizens who sought to preserve an attachment to Britain.

English in Canada

The spread of English to Canada was the consequence of colonies established by New Englanders in the eighteenth century, principally constituted of those who remained loyal to Britain following the American Declaration of Independence in 1776. At the same time, settlers arrived from England, Scotland, and Ireland, adding further dialects to the mixture. As a result, there are many similarities between the English heard in Canada and America, although Canadian English shares several features with the English spoken in the UK. In terms of pronunciation, Canadians tend to sound like Americans to most people from outside North America; distinctive features include the rhotic pronunciation of *car*, the 'd'-like pronunciation of *bottle*, and the use of American alternatives like 'tomayto' for British English 'tomahto', and 'skedule' for British English 'shedule'.

Canadian English does not follow American English in all such cases; British English preferences are found in words like *news*, which is pronounced 'nyoos' rather than 'noos', and in the pronunciation of *anti-*, where American English has 'antai'. While Canadian English follows American English in much of its vocabulary, compare *gas* (British English *petrol*), *sidewalk* (BrEng *pavement*), *trunk* (BrEng *boot*), it preserves English words such as *tap* (American English *faucet*), *cutlery* (American *silverware*), and *serviette* (American *napkin*). Canadian English spelling tends to follow British conventions, as in *honour*, *colour*, *centre*, and *theatre*, although some individual words, like *curb* and *tire*, follow the American practice.

English in Australia and New Zealand

The same process of dialect mixing that triggered a distinctive American variety lies behind the Englishes spoken in Australia and New Zealand. British convicts who were deported to Australia in the late eighteenth and nineteenth centuries were frequently of Cockney and Irish extraction, so that these dialects have a particular importance for the formation of the distinctive Australian accent. Colonial lag is evident in the preservation of some archaic English words, such as the Australian *tucker* 'food', from the word *tuck*, still preserved in old-fashioned English *tuck shops* and *tuck boxes*, and *dunny* 'toilet', which was current in English slang of the late eighteenth century.

Other features which are uniquely Australian are words formed by adding an 'ie' ending, as in *barbie* 'barbeque', *coldie* 'cold beer', *rellies* 'relatives', and even *Aussie*, as well as contractions like *arvo* 'afternoon', *journo* 'journalist', and *beaut* 'beauty'. British settlers in Australia adopted local words from Aboriginal languages to describe cultural objects and practices specific to Australia, such as the *boomerang*, from the Dharuk language, and indigenous animals such as *koala*, *wallaby*, and *kangaroo*.

Sadly, the story that the name of the kangaroo derives from the locals' bemused response, 'I do not know', when asked the name of the animal, appears to be entirely fictional; rather more prosaically, the word *kangaroo* comes from a native word *ganurru*. The word and the animal were introduced to the English in an account of Captain Cook's expedition of 1770. Shortly after this, during his tour of the

Hebrides, Dr Johnson is reputed to have performed an imitation of the animal, gathering up the tails of his coat to resemble a pouch and bounding across the room. Later voyages to Botany Bay brought English settlers into contact with Aboriginals who knew the kangaroo by the alternative name *patagaran*, but who subsequently adopted the word *kangaroo*. *Kangaroo*, therefore, is an interesting example of a word borrowed into one Aboriginal language from another, via European settlers.

The first settlers in New Zealand arrived in the 1790s, although official colonies were not established until 1840. Because this is a more recent variety, more is known about the dialects of the earliest settlers who first migrated from Britain to New Zealand. Recordings made in the 1940s of speakers born and raised in New Zealand reveal a liberal and apparently random conglomeration of features drawn from a great variety of English dialects. Greater affinity to Britain has led to the acceptance of more influence from the English spoken in Britain, while a desire to set the New Zealand usage apart from that of Australia has prompted further distinctive differences in accent. Where the Australian accent tends to pronounce the place name *Sydney* as 'Seedney', New Zealanders prefer a 'Sudney'-style pronunciation.

The influx of English speakers triggered a dramatic decline in the indigenous Maori language, which had been spoken by the Polynesian peoples who had settled the islands during the first millennium; the number of monoglot Maoris dropped by 75 per cent during the nineteenth century. While village schools instructed their pupils in Maori, this was a bridge to enable the acquisition of English literacy and culture, and by the early twentieth century the use of Maori had been officially outlawed in school playgrounds.

More recently, a willingness to embrace Maori culture has led to the deliberate adoption of words from the indigenous languages, especially in toponyms, such as *Otago*, from a Maori word meaning 'place of red ochre'. In some cases indigenous names are used alongside English ones: Mount Taranaki/Mount Egmont and Aoraki/Mount Cook. More common Maori loanwords have also been adopted into wider use, such as *puku* (stomach), *kai* (food), *ka pai* (good), *maunga* (mountain), *waka* (boat), *wai* (water), *wahine* (woman), and *kia ora* (hello); beyond a handful of words like *kiwi* and *haka*, few are known outside New Zealand. But, while the 1987 Maori Language Act gave English and Maori equal status as co-official languages, the relatively small number of Maori speakers (around 14 per cent of the total population of more than four million), combined with their relatively low social position, means that the language continues to be under threat.

Models

The dissemination of English linked to the expansion and domination of the British Empire is only part of the story of the language's progression across the globe. Today English is the primary language in some sixty countries and continues to spread, especially as a second language. A useful model to document the expansion of English today, developed by an Indian-American linguist, Braj B. Kachru, employs three concentric circles to reflect the different ways in which English continues to gain new speakers (see Figure 11).

The Inner Circle represents the English language's traditional heartland, USA, Canada, UK, Australia, and New Zealand, where it is spoken as a native tongue by some 350 million people. The Outer Circle comprises non-native countries where English has an important status as an official

Three concentric circles of Englishes

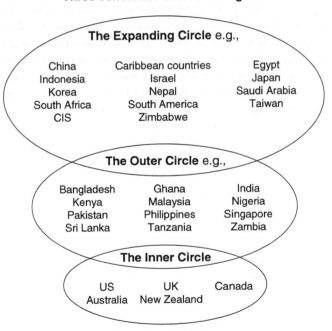

Figure 11 Kachru's model of global Englishes.

second language, including post colonial countries such as Singapore, Kenya, and India. The third concentric circle is termed the Expanding Circle: this encompasses all other countries where English is recognized as an international language, used in business and trade, but where it has no special status, nor a historical link with England through colonization, such as China and Japan.

We could view these colonial Englishes as offspring of the parent language, using a family-tree model similar to that developed by philologists reconstructing the relationships between older forms of language families. A limitation of such a model is that it assumes straight descent, making no allowance for influence between these varieties, such as the major role played by Scots and Irish speakers in the development of US, New Zealand, and Australian varieties. Another limitation of such a model is that it places the UK at the root of the tree. This may be historically accurate, but the centrality of British English is much less clear today. There are now far more speakers of English in the USA than in Britain, while the success of American popular culture and media, combined with its dominance as the language of the Internet, means that the English spoken in the USA has become increasingly influential.

Despite a long history of British prejudice against American English, which can be traced back to Dr Johnson, who viewed its influence as the sort of 'corruption to which every language widely diffused must always be exposed', Americanisms like *movie*, *cookie*, and *elevator*, its distinctive spellings such as *thru* and *donut*, phrases like 'Can I get a coffee', 'I'm good', and pronunciations like 'skedule' rather than 'shedule', are spreading across the globe.

The mixing of Englishes and the formation of distinctive new varieties is accelerated by its use among non-native speakers as a lingua franca. Such interactions tend to result in considerable 'code-switching'—a linguistic term that refers to the way speakers shift between their native languages and English in a conversation. This is perhaps most evident in South Asia, where there are huge numbers of speakers for whom English is their second language, though its status varies across the different constituent countries.

English in South Asia

The origins of South Asian English lie in Britain; the English language was established in India, Singapore, Malaysia, and Hong Kong as they were incorporated within the British Empire. During the period of British sovereignty in India, English was adopted as the principal language of administration, law, and education. Today, English retains official recognition as an associate language of India, alongside the main official language of Hindi, although in some areas it is the official language, while in others it is preferred to Hindi as a lingua franca. Since the population of India is in excess of a billion people, this creates the potential for a vast collection of English speakers, although the varying levels of education mean that the total number is closer to 250 million, with perhaps a further 350,000 using English as a second language.

A further 22 million people speak English as a second language in Pakistan, Nepal, Bangladesh, Bhutan, and Sri Lanka. English is used in Hong Kong, Singapore, and Malaysia as the medium for the education, legal, and administrative systems, though it is not accorded any form of official status. English enjoys a more central role in Singapore than in Malaysia, where Malay is dominant, or in Hong Kong, where Chinese has primary status.

Mixed Varieties: Singlish

The interaction between English and these Asian varieties has led to considerable language mixing; in Singapore, a new variety, known as Singlish, has emerged. While the Singaporean education system, its broadcasting corporation, and newspapers such as the *Strait Times* continue to recognize Standard British English and its RP accent, many Singaporeans employ a colloquial variety which mixes English with Malay and Chinese.

A characteristic instance of such mixing is the frequent use of the Chinese discourse particles *lah* and *ah*, tagged on to the ends of sentences to convey emphasis: 'Ok-lah', or to indicate a question: 'Should I go-ah?' Singlish incorporates loanwords, such as the Malay *makan* 'food', and Chinese *ang pow* 'cash gift', while words of English origin have different meanings, such as *send* 'take' and *stay* 'live'. Further distinctive features of Singlish include its tendency to drop articles, 'You have book?', plural inflexions, 'I have two car', verb endings, 'Yesterday I walk home', 'This taste good', and even the verb *to be*: 'This man clever' (see Figure 12).

Despite its widespread use, especially among the younger generation, the official status of Singlish continues to provoke controversy. The Singapore government remains firmly committed to the promotion of Standard English as the language of education, trade, commerce, and technology. In order to challenge the widespread use of Singlish, in 2000 the government launched the 'Speak Good English' campaign, which aimed to promote Standard English at the expense of Singlish, considered to be incomprehensible to outsiders.

Despite the appearance of Chinglish, Japlish, Denglish, Anglikaans, and other mixed varieties, or 'interlanguages', their status continues to be hotly debated. Are they

Figure 12 Advertisement in Singlish. Pulai Ubin, Singapore.

examples of 'code-switching', pidgins, or dialects that have borrowed significantly from another language?

The mixed variety called Chicano English, popularly known as Spanglish, is a well-established dialect widely used among the more than 44 million members of America's Hispanic population, alongside several other Spanish-influenced dialects. Since it is spoken as a first language by people who are not bilinguals of Spanish and English, and has its own radio stations, TV talk shows, advertisements, and magazines, Chicano English has a strong case for being considered a language in its own right. Yet while many of its native speakers praise its flexibility and expressiveness, traditionalists continue to cast it in socially divisive terms as an 'invasion' of one language by another.

In former colonies, the appropriation and remodelling represented by mixed forms of English have political and ideological ramifications. Where the Standard English of Britain is linked with a nation's colonial past, mixed forms of English come to stand for greater political and national independence. As the novelist Salman Rushdie has written: 'Those peoples who were once colonized by the language are now rapidly remaking it, domesticating it, becoming more and more relaxed about the way they use it. Assisted by the English language's flexibility and size, they are carving out large territories for themselves within its front.' The reappropriation and remodelling of English that is apparent in such mixed varieties, driven by communicative and ideological factors, is likely to play a major role in the language's future development.

Pidgins and Creoles

The kind of language mixing represented by Singlish is often labelled 'pidgin English'—a term used popularly to describe unsuccessful attempts to speak English. In linguistics, pidgin English is a neutral term that refers to a simplified version of English spoken by people for whom English is not their native language. An English pidgin acts as a kind of lingua franca, used for specific and restricted purposes, such as carrying out international trade and business. Because of this, pidgins tend to emerge along trade routes, as happened along the western coast of Africa, or in the Caribbean and Pacific Islands. English-based pidgins are still found today in Australia, West Africa, the Solomon Islands, and Papua New Guinea.

The term *pidgin* is thought to derive from an attempt by Chinese speakers to reproduce the English word *business*, so that etymologically *pidgin English* means 'business English'. The process of pidginization occurs when a simplified version of a language comes to be used for a limited set of functions—such as in the world of business. As a result, the dominant, or 'superstrate', language generally undergoes simplification, and is often influenced by the native, or 'substrate', language(s) of its speakers, so that the resulting language presents a considerable admixture of features.

Although such languages are frequently dismissed as being unsuccessful attempts to speak English, or corruptions of English, they are neither. Criticisms of the 'corrupt' English spoken by colonial societies can be traced back to the nineteenth century; the 'barbarous idiom' employed by

Jamaican natives was presented as evidence both of their inferior racial status and the threat they posed to British society and cultural values. The concept of pidgin English was actively cultivated in nineteenth-century Britain and the USA in order construct a racially prejudiced image of the Chinese among westerners.

However, like any other language, a pidgin can develop a consistent structure of its own. Although it is based upon features taken from several distinct languages, this is no different from Standard English, which has borrowed liberally from other languages throughout its history. Where a pidgin language begins to be learned by children as their first language, it acquires full language status and is termed a *creole*, from a French word meaning 'indigenous'. The technical distinction between a pidgin and a creole, therefore, is that the latter has native speakers.

Some scholars have suggested that pidgins provide insights into the processes of linguistic evolution; but others dispute this, arguing that far from being evidence of the evolutionary process, a pidgin represents a corruption of a true language. It is true that pidgins are simplified languages that must develop into creoles before they can begin the development back to a full language. But pidgins should not be confused with the kind of spontaneous corruption caused by a speaker trying to communicate in a language for which he or she has only the most basic competence, even though they may have their origins in such attempts.

Although it may not be apparent to a speaker of Standard English unfamiliar with a pidginized variety, pidgins employ structures which must be learned—albeit more straightforwardly than a language like German or French—and which cannot simply be improvised. Where a pidgin tends to adopt vocabulary items from the superstrate language—English in the cases we are discussing here—its grammatical structure usually derives from the substrate language.

Tok Pisin (literally 'talk pidgin') is the name given to the English-based creole used in Papua New Guinea, formed in the nineteenth century between English traders and speakers of indigenous languages in the South Pacific. It is related to Pijin, spoken in the Solomon Islands, and Bislama, spoken in Vanuatu. Since Papua New Guinea is home to some 750 different indigenous languages, Tok Pisin has served an invaluable role in enabling communication between communities. It was not until the 1960s, however, that it began to be acquired by children as a native tongue.

Since the grammatical structure of Tok Pisin appears a crude simplification of that of English, with features common to the language spoken by children, it was long dismissed as unworthy of serious study. Tok Pisin uses the pronoun *mi* as the subject pronoun—an error frequently committed by children and frowned upon by purists (see Chapter 5). But its grammatical structure is more complicated than this suggests. For instance, possessive constructions are formed by adding the word *bilong* 'belong'; the equivalent of *my father* in Tok Pisin is therefore *papa bilong mi*. Plurals are formed by adding the suffix 'pela', derived from the English word *fellow*: thus the second-person singular pronoun *yu* has a plural equivalent *yupela*. The reintroduction of a number distinction in the second-person pronoun shows that a pidgin is not necessarily grammatically less sophisticated than a full language, since *yupela* enables a distinction which has not been possible in Standard English since the second-person singular pronoun *thou* became obsolete (see Chapter 5).

Because scholars dismissed pidgins and creoles as unfit for serious study, little was recorded about how and why such languages came into being. An older view that attributed their simplified structure to the inferior intellectual abilities of primitive societies has now been dismissed, since it has been shown that the languages of such communities are just as developed as those of more advanced civilizations, albeit often with a more limited lexicon.

An alternative theory proposes that pidginization began when native speakers deliberately simplified their speech in order to aid communication, in the same way as a contemporary speaker does when giving directions to a tourist today, or as a parent does to a child. The non-native speaker responds in a similar way, unaware that this form of the language is a drastic simplification. According to a modified version of this theory, based on the assumption that in a master–slave relationship the native speaker is unlikely to accommodate in this way, the pidgin is considered to be the result of an imperfect learning of the language, exacerbated by a lack of feedback and correction.

The Future

Given this narrative of constant expansion, language mixing, and new dialect formation, we might wonder what the future is for English in the twenty-first century. Will its continued spread lead to further fragmentation, so that future speakers of English around the globe will no longer be able to understand each other?

Despite the efforts of the Singaporean government, Singlish continues to flourish. As new generations grow up preferring mixed tongues like Singlish in the home, the playground, and on the streets, so these varieties will begin to supplant Standard English in the more formal and prestigious domains. While Standard English retains an important international function in Singapore, Singlish plays a key role in the establishment of a national identity and in negotiating and maintaining interpersonal relationships. The displacement of Standard English in official use in its former colonies would inevitably lead to greater divisions between the English of the Inner Circle and that used in the Expanding Circle. Would such varieties remain mutually intelligible under such conditions?

One way of predicting the future might be to look back at the past. The dominance of English today has parallels in the role of Latin in pre-modern Europe. Having been spread by the success of the Roman Empire, Classical Latin continued to be employed as a standard written variety throughout much of Europe long after the fall of the Roman Empire. But once it had lost its population of native speakers, Classical Latin became an artificial and learned written variety, increasingly divorced from the Vulgar Latin used in speech. The spoken language continued to change, resulting in the emergence of new dialects, the ancestors of the Romance languages: French, Spanish,

Portuguese, Romanian, and Italian. Might the future witness a similar break up of English into a series of mutually-incomprehensible Englishes? If this were to happen, would these languages be English, or something else entirely?

But while the analogy with Latin is a useful one, there are clear differences. Where Classical Latin fell out of use entirely in seventeenth-century Europe, Standard English continues to occupy a prominent role on the global stage. As long as English retains its significance in important domains such as the United Nations, the European Community, science and technology, and the entertainment industry, it will preserve its dominant status as a world language. While Classical Latin struggled on as a language without native speakers, Standard English remains the variety used in writing by some 450 million people. Whatever the success of the Singapore government's Good English campaign, it does at least serve to highlight the enduring status and prestige of Standard English.

An alternative projection into the future might predict that, rather than witness the break up of Standard English, the following centuries will see Standard English function as a unifying force, just as Classical Latin did into the seventeenth century—long after its spoken varieties had broken up into distinct dialects—enabling it to function as a lingua franca (in writing at least) for a long time after its demise as a native language. Despite ceasing to be a mother tongue in AD 400, Classical Latin continued to be learned, and persisted as the language of religious, scholarly, and historical discourse throughout Europe until the end of the seventeenth century, enabling scholarly, diplomatic, and religious writings to traverse national boundaries. A similar role could be filled by Standard English in the future, enabling and facilitating communication, rather than standing in its way.

Linguists have detected the emergence of a variety known as World Standard English in use throughout the globe, which may lend qualified support to such a theory. Although not a single, fixed variety, World Standard English appears to be operating as a regionally neutral and increasingly uniform standard, available for use by English speakers of any nation. In its written form, this standard draws upon American conventions of spelling; in chemistry we find *sulfur* rather than *sulphur*, in computing we find *program* not *programme*, *disk* not *disc*. In the spoken language it remains unclear whether the British prestige RP accent or the General American accent will come to be recognized as a single agreed standard. A further possibility is that it will be neither British English nor General American that will be selected, but rather a kind of compromise variety that draws on both, and potentially other, Englishes. A possible model for this is the 'Euro-English' that can be heard within the European Parliament among representatives from throughout the European Union.

Predictions about the break-up of the English language into distinct languages are not new. Writing in 1877, the linguist Henry Sweet (the inspiration behind Bernard Shaw's Henry Higgins) asserted that in a hundred years: 'England, America, and Australia will be speaking mutually unintelligible languages.' While Sweet's confident forecast warns us against attempting to predict the future, it also reminds us that gloomy prophecies about the end of English as we know it are not new, and do not necessarily come true.

7

Why Do We Care?

'"You seemed to find one or two of the reports very interesting, sir." "Did I?" Morse sounded surprised. "You spent about ten minutes on that one from the secretarial college, and it's only half a page." "You're very observant, Lewis, but I'm sorry to disappoint you. It was the most ill-written report I've seen in years, with twelve—no less—grammatical monstrosities in ten lines! What's the force coming to?"' (Colin Dexter, *Last Bus to Woodstock*, 1975, p. 33).

Why would a busy Chief Inspector spend his time scrutinizing, counting, and correcting the grammatical mistakes in the reports submitted to him, rather than focusing on their contents? Why should the sloppy grammar of a missive from the secretarial college provoke Morse into despair for the future of the police force? Why do we care about grammar and spelling to the extent that minor errors trigger paroxysms of despondency and gloom concerning the future of our society and its language?

Rights and Wrongs

Since most people recognize the inevitability of linguistic change, or are at least aware that Shakespeare's language differs from our own, we might wonder why they are unwilling to allow the language to continue to change today. One answer to this question lies in the fact that, as users of English, it is impossible for us to take an external stance from which to observe current usage. As we have all had to acquire the English language, negotiating its grammatical niceties, its fiendishly tricky spellings, and its unusual pronunciations, it is impossible for us to adopt a neutral position from which to observe debates concerning correct usage. In his soapbox rant against sloppy grammar and poor spelling, comedian David Mitchell confesses: 'I'm certainly happy to admit that I do have a huge vested interest in upholding these rules because I did take the trouble to learn them and, having put that effort in, I am abundantly incentivized to make sure that everyone else follows suit.'

This point is well articulated by the linguists James and Lesley Milroy, who contend that 'All social actors view the sociolinguistic world from the perspective characteristic of their group. *There is no absolutely neutral perspective—no view from nowhere.*' Different social and educational circumstances create alternative perspectives from which to judge what is correct, or 'ordinary', usage, as we see in this exchange in D. H. Lawrence's novel *Lady Chatterley's Lover*

(1928) between Lady Constance Chatterley and her game-keeper Mellors, who speaks with a broad Derbyshire dialect:

> "Appen yer'd better 'ave this key, an' Ah mun fend for t'bods some other road'...
> She looked at him, getting his meaning through the fog of the dialect.
> 'Why don't you speak ordinary English?' she said coldly.
> 'Me! Ah thowt it wor ordinary'.

Conventions of correct usage are drummed into us early in our lives, by parents and schoolteachers, and it is very difficult to shake these off in adulthood. Even professional linguists struggle to do so. Deborah Cameron, author of *Verbal Hygiene*, a study of linguistic prescriptivism, observes that as a professional linguist she has learned to overcome knee-jerk value judgements that are inappropriate in this field of study. But, despite this, she still finds herself sensitive to particular solecisms: 'I can choose to suppress the irritation I feel when I see, for example, a sign that reads "Potatoe's"; I cannot choose not to feel it.'

Mary Schmich, writing in the *Chicago Tribune* following Barack Obama's apparent misuse of the word *enormity* in his presidential acceptance speech of 2008 (see Chapter 3), found herself wincing as she recalled her sixth-grade teacher, Miss Birch, shouting 'Enormity does not mean it's big'; Schmich writes: 'Because I was browbeaten in my formative years by such language warriors, I felt called to crusade to restore "enormity" to its proper meaning: "monstrous wickedness".' Despite the unpleasant and intimidating way in which this 'proper' meaning was drilled into her as a child by a bullying teacher, this writer has unquestioningly adopted its premise, along with a compulsion to impose it upon others.

Much of the success of style guides may be credited to society's tacit acceptance that there are rights and wrongs in all aspects of usage, and a desire to be saved from embarrassment. Rather than question the grounds for the prescription, we turn to usage pundits as we once turned to our schoolteachers, in search of guidance and certitude. In a fast-changing and uncertain world, there is something reassuring about knowing that the values of our schooldays continue to be upheld, and that the correct placement of an apostrophe still matters.

Good Grammar in the Marketplace

Another reason for our concern with such pedantry is bound up with the social cachet that surrounds the concept of 'good grammar'. The commercial potential of 'good grammar' can be observed in the way that companies deliberately invoke notions of correctness to appeal to an educated and wealthy demographic. Why else would the supermarket chain Tesco feel compelled to bow to public demand and reword the '10 items or less' signs that accompany their supermarket checkouts? The change to 'Up to 10 items' was implemented following pressure from the Plain English campaign, who claim that the revised sign is 'easy to understand and avoids any debate'. But was there ever any confusion with the former wording? How many people were really objecting to the signs on the grounds that they were unable to calculate how many items they were permitted to take to the checkout? If they were, the new signs are unlikely to clarify matters, since it might reasonably be inferred that up to 10 items means 9 rather than 10.

Simply avoiding the stigmatized '10 items or less' will not satisfy true pedants, for whom the only correct version would read '10 items or fewer' (see Figure 13). This is because, according to the rules of correct grammar, *fewer* should be used of count nouns, and *less* of mass (non-countable) nouns. The value of maintaining such standards in an attempt to appeal to a particular kind of customer is well understood by Waitrose, whose signs read '10 Items or Fewer.' Responding to this wording, one blogger writes: 'From now on, I shall only ever be shopping in Waitrose. I love you Waitrose. I really, really love you.' It is hard to imagine the same emotional response being triggered by 'Up to 10 items.' By using *fewer*, Waitrose is sending a message of solidarity to its customers that says 'we care about the same things as you do', while simultaneously allowing its customers the chance to feel a sense of social and intellectual smugness and superiority.

But, while Waitrose may appear to be bravely upholding an important grammatical distinction in a world that has ceased to care for such matters, the basis for this so-called rule is especially flimsy. As with many of the grammatical prescriptions we have met in this book, its origins lie in the eighteenth century. It was first formulated by Robert Baker in his *Reflections on the English Language: Being a Detection of many improper Expressions used in Conversation, and of many others to be found in Authors* (1770), where he writes of *less*:

"What can I say? I was an English major."

Figure 13 Fewer or less?

'This Word is most commonly used in speaking of a Number; where I should think Fewer would do better. No fewer than a Hundred appears to me not only more elegant than No less than a Hundred, but more strictly proper.' It is clear from the wording of this statement that, far from setting down a hard and fast rule to be followed for hundreds of years to come, Baker is simply expressing a personal preference based on his subjective ideas of stylistic elegance. Most significantly, he was certainly not basing his statement on previous practice, since *less* had been used of countable nouns since Old English times.

While the distinction between *fewer* and *less* remains sacrosanct for some people today, there are others who are oblivious to such nuances of usage. When it comes to amounts of money, distance, and time this rule does not apply. We say less than 10 miles, less than 10 minutes, less than 10 pounds. Since supermarket checkouts refer to the total amount of items, it is perfectly acceptable to say 10 items or less.

Following Waitrose's lead, other retailers have looked to cash in on the marketability of grammatical correctness. The London department store Selfridges went as far as inviting N. M. Gwynne to offer in-store grammar classes to its shoppers (though not far enough for the Apostrophe Protection Society, which has campaigned for the reinsertion of the apostrophe into the name of the department store).

But, while good grammar may appeal to a particular kind of customer, companies wishing to connect with a younger demographic deliberately contravene such conventions. Thus the restaurant chain McDonald's drops the 'g' in its slogan 'I'm lovin' it', though it replaces it with an apostrophe so as not to alienate its older and more traditional customer base. Apple Macintosh's 1997 slogan 'Think Different', instead of the grammatically correct 'Think Differently', uses non-standard grammar to signal its willingness to stand apart from the crowd and to appeal to a more modern, laid-back customer base. Where good grammar is seen to enshrine and maintain traditional social hierarchies, non-standard grammar consciously undermines and challenges them.

Good Grammar in the Classroom

For many, good grammar is a cipher for other social values, such as politeness, respect, and the preservation of traditional social mores. For them, the dropping of formal grammar teaching in schools is directly responsible for the breakdown in social hierarchies, youth unemployment, crime, and many other social ills. In the 1980s, a move away from formal grammar teaching in English secondary schools was cited by some social commentators as the trigger for a widespread disregard for honesty and responsibility among young people.

In an interview on Radio 4 in 1985, Conservative MP Norman Tebbit linked standards of English with standards of dress and hygiene, and levels of honesty and law-abidance: 'If you allow standards to slip to the stage where good English is no better than bad English, where people turn up filthy at school . . . all these things tend to cause people to have no standards at all, and once you lose standards then there's no imperative to stay out of crime.'

In 2009, Prince Charles, a long-standing advocate of the teaching of grammar, made an explicit link between the values of 'balance and harmony' and the rediscovery of 'the book of grammar, chucked out of the window in the twentieth century'. Such comments tend to reflect a misunderstanding of what the formal teaching of grammar actually involves, or exactly what kinds of knowledge have been lost. In such debates, 'grammar' represents a particular set of educational values—ones that employ traditional methods like rote learning and formal examinations.

A key factor in the rejection of grammatical study in English schools in the twentieth century was the rise of English literature as a discipline. As a subject concerned with cultivating critical awareness, artistic taste, and literary sensibilities, the scientific study of the language (initially known as *philology*) was felt to be irrelevant to English Studies.

The reintroduction of formal grammatical teaching in the 1980s was accompanied by a shift from a prescriptivist to a descriptivist methodology. Where previous approaches to grammar teaching had drilled children to avoid 'errors' such as *I was stood*, the new curriculum encouraged an appreciation of dialectal and non-standard varieties alongside the acquisition of Standard English. For many traditionalists, this permissive approach represents a watering-down of the subject and a lowering of educational standards, accompanied by a loss of valued teaching methods, such as grammatical parsing, memorization, and rote learning. The benefits of such approaches over what he disparagingly refers to as a 'Modern "child-centred" education theory' is stressed by N. M. Gwynne, who urges his readers to learn his grammatical definitions '*exactly* by heart, including even their word order'.

Good Grammar and Latin Grammar

The dropping of grammar from the English curriculum in the 1960s coincided with a decline in the teaching of Classics in English schools. Once English grammar was reintroduced with the National Curriculum in 1988, this was seen by some as an opportunity to revive the formal grammatical description that had previously been the province of Latin and Greek.

Throughout its history, the codification of the rules of correct grammar has been closely linked with the teaching of classical languages. We saw in Chapter 4 how eighteenth-century grammarians modelled their accounts of English grammar upon that of Latin. The prestige of Latin has continued to infect accounts of English grammar up to the present day. H. W. Fowler, whose *Modern English Usage* (1926) was the most influential usage guide of the twentieth century, read Classics at Oxford and spent some time as a Classics teacher before turning to lexicography. His linguistic prescriptions are soaked through with edicts derived from Latin grammar. The Latin use of the nominative case following the verb *to be* prompts Fowler to condemn English constructions such as *it is me*; according to Fowler, this 'false grammar' should properly be *it is I*. Fowler's prescription continues to find loyal adherents today; ironically, it is probably to blame for the widespread overcompensation (or 'hypercorrection') which leads to the preference for incorrect *I* in phrases such as 'between you and me'.

Fowler defended his reliance upon Latin models against criticisms from the Danish linguist Otto Jespersen by arguing that 'our grammatical conscience has by this time a Latin element inextricably compounded in it'. Note how Fowler appeals here not to linguistic facts but to a 'grammatical conscience', suggesting that the influence of Latin occupies a different order of importance for English speakers than a purely linguistic one.

As we have seen, many of our ideas of linguistic correctness were established in the eighteenth century. During this period, concerns for linguistic corruption and correctness were triggered by the establishment of new social hierarchies and anxieties. The admiration for the Latin language, which for centuries had been the language of the Church and European scholarship, led to the assumption that synthetic languages—those which rely upon inflexional endings to carry grammatical information—were of a higher order than analytical ones—languages that make comparatively little use of such endings—leading to a more efficient and effective mode of communication. Since earlier stages of English employed inflexions more than later ones, the history of English was viewed as a process of corruption and decay.

Since Latin had not been a living language (one with native speakers) for centuries, it existed in a fixed form; by contrast, English was unstable and in decline. This view of Latin as a unified and fixed entity perseveres today, encouraged by the way modern textbooks present a single variety (usually that of Cicero), suppressing the wide variation attested in original Latin writings. Since the eighteenth century, efforts to outlaw variation and to introduce greater fixity in English have been driven by a desire to emulate the model of this prestigious classical forebear. N. M. Gwynne overtly links mastery of English grammar with a solid foundation in the Latin language, advising his readers to turn next to a Latin primer, which is now conveniently available in *Gwynne's Latin* (2014).

The Marketability of Good Grammar

The success of the Gwynne franchise leads me nicely to a further reason why people continue to care about good grammar: it sells. Despite its idiosyncrasies of coverage and approach, *Fowler's Modern English Usage* was a bestseller: in the preface to his revised edition of 1965, Ernest Gowers estimated that the first edition had sold more than half a million copies. The huge demand for such books can be traced back to the beginnings of the prescriptive tradition in the eighteenth century. From just a handful of grammars issuing from the presses in the sixteenth and seventeenth centuries, there was a huge increase to over two hundred such works published in the eighteenth century.

Perhaps the most notable of recent commercial successes was the runaway bestseller *Eats, Shoots & Leaves: The Zero Tolerance Approach to Punctuation* (2003) by Lynne Truss. Truss' appeal to fellow sticklers to fight back against sloppiness and falling standards of punctuation sold several million copies in the UK. Is the British public really so concerned about where to put a comma or a semi-colon? More plausibly, the book's success was due to its function as a rallying cry to a generation concerned about a perceived lack of respect for traditional social mores among young people. It is no coincidence that it was followed up by the publication of *Talk to the Hand*, a book bemoaning the rudeness of modern society.

English and Nationalism

Eats, Shoots & Leaves achieved commercial success in the USA too, despite a cool reception in the pages of *The New Yorker*, where Louis Menand took issue with the book's own punctuation, concluding that 'an Englishwoman lecturing Americans on semicolons is a little like an American lecturing the French on sauces'. This comment reveals how concern for the language can be made to stand proxy for a concern for the country.

Nationalistic sentiments have been invoked as part of efforts to make English the official language of the USA by the English-only movement, which claims that such a move would further integration and unity. Critics of the movement have opposed its intolerance of other languages, accusing its supporters of being driven more by a desire to further the segregation and marginalization of non-English speakers than a wish to achieve racial and political unity.

Complaints by Nigel Farage, leader of the UK Independence Party, about the dominance of foreign-language speakers in British schools are evidence of how the status of the English language in Britain has been politicized in the debate over immigration. Is the status of English really under threat in Britain and the USA, or is the true agenda here a concern with limiting the numbers and rights of immigrants? Responding to the claims of the English-only movement in the USA, linguist Geoffrey Pullum suggested that making English the official language is as necessary as making hotdogs the official food at baseball games.

If the global status of English seems assured, so does the future of the age-old antagonism between descriptivists and prescriptivists. Despite this binary opposition representing a considerable simplification of both positions, it serves a useful purpose for the media and usage pundits who like to provoke prescriptivists by portraying professional linguists, for whom any error is apparently simply evidence of linguistic variation and change, as opponents of literacy standards. Since most professional linguists are themselves educators, required to instruct their pupils in the conventions of standard written English, this is an extreme characterization of their position.

News stories that seek to stir up outrage towards the latest edition of a dictionary tend to paint a similarly black and white picture. In reports of the *OED*'s revised entry for *literally* (discussed in Chapter 3), journalists ignored the label which marks this usage as non-standard, instead casting the debate as a simple choice between right and wrong.

The dismissive manner in which professional linguists have typically ignored prescriptivist approaches has also contributed to the lack of dialogue and continued misinformation. Since prescriptivist approaches are widely held and have a demonstrable impact upon the use of English and its future, it is clearly incumbent upon professional linguists to accord its proponents due attention and to engage in public debate. Hopefully (or, as some would prefer, it is to be hoped that) this book will help to stimulate and inform such dialogue.

FURTHER READING

Jean Aitchison, *Language Change: Progress or Decay?*, 4th edition (Cambridge: Cambridge University Press, 2012).

Kingsley Amis, *The King's English* (London: Penguin, 2001).

Richard Bailey, *Speaking American: A History of English in the United States* (Oxford: Oxford University Press, 2012).

Charles Barber, Joan C. Beal, and Philip A. Shaw, *The English Language: A Historical Introduction*, 2nd edition (Cambridge: Cambridge University Press, 2009).

Deborah Cameron, *Verbal Hygiene*, 2nd edition (Abingdon: Routledge, 2012).

Tom Chatfield, *Netymology: From Apps to Zombies: A Linguistic Celebration of the Digital World* (London: Quercus, 2013).

David Crystal (ed.), *Samuel Johnson, A Dictionary of the English Language: An Anthology* (London: Penguin, 2005).

David Crystal, *The Stories of English* (London: Penguin, 2005).

David Crystal, *The Fight for English: How Language Pundits Ate, Shot, and Left* (Oxford: Oxford University Press, 2006).

David Crystal, *Language and the Internet*, 2nd edition (Cambridge: Cambridge University Press, 2006).

David Crystal, *Txtng: The Gr8 Db8* (Oxford: Oxford University Press, 2008).

H. W. Fowler, *Modern English Usage* (Oxford: Oxford University Press, 1926); 2nd edition, Ernest Gowers (Oxford: Oxford University Press, 1965); 3rd edition, R. W. Burchfield (Oxford: Oxford University Press, 1996); 4th edition, Jeremy Butterfield (Oxford: Oxford University Press, 2015).

N. M. Gwynne, *Gwynne's Grammar: The Ultimate Introduction to Grammar and the Writing of Good English* (London: Ebury Press, 2013).

N. M. Gwynne, *Gwynne's Latin: The Ultimate Introduction to Latin* (London: Ebury Press, 2014).

Simon Heffer, *Strictly English: The Correct Way to Write . . . and Why it Matters* (London: Windmill, 2011).

Henry Hitchings, *Dr Johnson's Dictionary: The Extraordinary Story of the Book that Defined the World* (London: John Murray, 2005).

Henry Hitchings, *The Secret Life of Words: How English Became English* (London: John Murray, 2008).

Henry Hitchings, *The Language Wars: A History of Proper English* (London: John Murray, 2011).

John Honey, *Does Accent Matter? The Pygmalion Factor* (London: Faber, 1989).

Simon Horobin, *Does Spelling Matter?* (Oxford: Oxford University Press, 2013).

Keith Houston, *Shady Characters: Ampersands, Interrobangs and other Typographical Curiosities* (London: Particular Books, 2013).

Seth Lerer, *Inventing English: A Portable History of the Language* (New York: Columbia University Press, 2007).

Tim William Machan, *Language Anxiety: Conflict and Change in the History of English* (Oxford: Oxford University Press, 2009).

David Marsh, *For Who the Bell Tolls: One Man's Quest for Grammatical Perfection* (London: Guardian and Faber, 2013).

Tom McArthur, *The English Languages* (Cambridge: Cambridge University Press, 1998).

James Milroy and Lesley Milroy, *Authority in Language: Investigating Standard English*, 4th edition (London: Routledge, 2012).

Lynda Mugglestone, *Talking Proper: The Rise of Accent as Social Symbol*, 2nd edition (Oxford: Oxford University Press, 2003).

Lynda Mugglestone, *Dictionaries: A Very Short Introduction* (Oxford: Oxford University Press, 2011).

George Orwell, *Politics and the English Language* (London: Penguin, 2013).

Ammon Shea, *Bad English: A History of Linguistic Aggravation* (New York: Penguin, 2014).

Ishtla Singh, *Pidgins and Creoles: An Introduction* (London: Routledge, 2000).

Peter Trudgill, *Sociolinguistics: An Introduction to Language and Society*, 4th edition (London: Penguin 2000).

Lynne Truss, *Eats, Shoots & Leaves: The Zero Tolerance Approach to Punctuation* (London: Profile, 2003).

Clive Upton and John Widdowson, *Survey of English Dialects: the Dictionary and Grammar* (London: Routledge, 1994).

Clive Upton and John Widdowson, *An Atlas of English Dialects* (Oxford: Oxford University Press, 1996; revised edition, 2006).

ELECTRONIC RESOURCES

BBC Voices Project: <http://www.bbc.co.uk/voices/>

British Library Sounds: Accents and dialects: <http://sounds.bl.uk/Accents-and-dialects>

Dictionary of American Regional English: <http://www.daredictionary.com>

Oxford English Dictionary: <http://www.oed.com>

INDEX

Académie Française 47, 121–2
academies 46–9
accent 6, 72, 74–7, 82–9, 101, 105, 106–7, 108, 132, 136, 137, 142, 151
acronyms 42, 120, 123
Adams, John 48, 134
adorkable 39, 68, 69
affixation 18, 37, 122
African American English 78–9, 110
aggravate 66
agreement 20
ain't 44–6, 108
aitch 53–4
American Heritage Dictionary 42, 46
Amis, Kingsley 64, 66
Anglo-Norman 28
Apostrophe Protection Society 158
Apple Macintosh 159
Arabic 14, 32
archaism 4, 27, 61, 133, 136
Auden, W. H. 92
Australia 140

Baker, Robert 156
bangorrhea 126
Barnes, William 10
BBC 72, 87–8, 108

BBC Voices Project 112–13
Bede 20–2
blends 78, 120, 122–3
Boswell, James 103
Bridges, Robert 48–9
Bullokar, William 95
Burchfield, R. W. 53
Bush, George W. 39
Butterfield, Jeremy 53–4

Cædmon 21
Cameron, Deborah 154
Canada 135
capital letters 36, 126, 129
Carroll, Lewis 122–3
case 19, 20, 26, 37, 93, 94, 111, 161
Cassidy, Frederic 116
Cawdrey, Robert 40–2
Caxton, William 81
Celtic 20–3
Chaucer, Geoffrey 29, 32, 58, 59, 64
Cheke, Sir John 9
Chesterfield, Lord 40, 56, 69
Chicano English 110, 144
Chinese 14, 142, 145
chronic 66

Cicero 163
Cockney 88–9, 118, 136
Cockney rhymes 107
code-switching 141, 144
Collins English Dictionary 39, 68
colonial lag 133, 136
colonization 32, 138–40
comparatives 61, 64
compounds 18, 23, 37, 38
Concise Oxford Dictionary 50
conversion 18, 124
Cooke, Thomas 95
creoles 8, 145–8
Crystal, David 127

Danish 17, 100, 104
decimate 66
definite article 20
Defoe, Daniel 47, 105–6
Dexter, Colin 152
dialect 6–7, 54, 72, 74–80, 81, 83,
    95, 99–100, 101–4, 105–6
Dickens, Charles 85
dictionaries 40–6, 50, 65
*Dictionary of American Regional
    English* 116–17
*Dictionary of the Older Scottish
    Tongue* 103
Dictionary of the Scots Language 103
dilemma 66
disinterested 39
Doric 103
double negatives 62–4, 90, 108
Dryden, John 47, 62, 64
Dutch 6, 17, 32, 100, 104, 133

Early Modern English 4–5, 30–2,
    111, 133
Ebonics 78–9
Egelsham, Wells 93
electronic discourse 120–30

Elements of Style, The 54
Eliot, T. S. 66
Ellis, Alexander 85–6
Ellis, Stanley 114
emoji 128–9
emoticon 123, 128
English Dialect Society 114
enormity 66–7, 154–5
Estuary English 88–9, 113, 118
etymology 65–7, 121
Euro English 13, 151
Evelyn, John 47
exclamation marks 126–9

Facebook 122, 124
Farage, Nigel 164–5
fewer 155–8
firstly 55
Fitzgerald, F. Scott 127
forms of address 70–1, 119
Forsyth, Mark 60, 92
Fowler, H. W. 45–6, 50–3, 55, 64,
    66, 121, 127–8, 161–3
French 14, 17, 27–31, 34–5,
    102, 133
Frisian 17
full-stop 126

Gaelic 102
garage 39, 87
German 17, 18, 37, 100, 104, 133
Germanic 17–20, 37, 100, 122
gerundives 95
gerunds 95
Gill, Alexander 105
glottaling 89
Gothic 17
Gowers, Ernest 53, 163
grammar 1, 8, 11, 50, 52, 61–4, 72,
    75, 86, 90–8, 102, 107–11, 130,
    152, 155–63

grammatical gender 19–20, 26, 37
Great Vowel Shift 32–3, 35, 101–2
Greek 10, 30, 31, 33–5, 38, 41, 65,
    99, 121, 161
greengrocer's apostrophe 36–7
Greenwood, James 64
Grimm's Law 17
Gwynne, Neville 158
Gwynne's Grammar 54, 55, 62, 74,
    94, 160–1
Gwynne's Latin 163

h-dropping 84–5
hashtag 121
Heffer, Simon 63, 64, 67, 69–70
Henderson, Michael 89
Hewes, John 93
Hindi 141
Honey, John 77
Humphrys, John 120
Hussain, Nassar 89
hypercorrection 162
hypothetic reconstruction 15

Icelandic 17
idiom 52
Indo-European 15–17, 19
inflexions 19, 25–6, 37, 110,
    142, 162
initialisms 123
interlanguages 143–4
interrobang 127
Irish 20
Italian 2, 17, 32

Jamieson, John 103
Jespersen, Otto 162
Johnson, Samuel 1, 2, 40–1, 56–7,
    65, 69, 81–2, 103, 124,
    137, 140
Jones, Daniel 87

Jonson, Ben 62
jouring 105

Kachru, Braj B. 138–9
Keats, John 107
kinship terms 17, 18, 25, 29

Labov, William 118–19
Lallans 104
Late Modern English 33–6
Latin 2, 14, 17, 20, 23–4, 29–32,
    33–5, 38, 41, 93, 149–50,
    161–3
Lawrence, D. H. 153–4
levelling 113, 118
literally 42–4, 52, 165
logic 61, 62–5
logograms 123
Lowth, Robert 96

malapropism 83
Malay 142
manuscripts 21, 26, 36, 81
Maori 137–8
Marsh, David 97–8
McDonald's 158
meh 39
Melville, Herman 129
Menand, Louis 164
Middle English 27–30, 31, 33, 75,
    80, 101, 102, 105, 109,
    132–3
Milton, John 56, 58, 59
Minor, Dr W. C. 57
minuscule 39
Mitchell, David 49, 153
Mockney 88–9
Modern English Usage see Fowler,
    H. W.
motherese 119
Mulcaster, Richard 131

Index

Murray, James 57
Mx 70–1
My Fair Lady 84

National Curriculum 161
New Zealand 129, 137–8, 140
Newton, Sir Isaac 30–1
Norman Conquest 3, 27–8, 30, 122
Norwegian 17, 24, 100, 102, 104
number 19, 26, 37

Obama, Barack 67, 154
Old English 2, 3–5, 9, 15, 17–18,
    20–7, 37, 57, 122
Old Norse 6, 24–6, 28
Orton, Harold 114
Orwell, George 10, 60
Oxford English Dictionary 39,
    42–3, 52, 53, 57–9, 68, 104, 122,
    123, 165

Palin, Sarah 39
parataxis 5
Partridge, Eric 55
Persian 32
philology 74, 160
Pickles, Wilfred 88
Pictish 20
pidgins 8, 13, 144, 145–8
Pinker, Steven 42, 46
Plain English 10, 155
Pocket Oxford Dictionary 50
political correctness 70
Pope, Alexander 62, 64
Portuguese 133, 150
prepositions 3, 6, 24, 90, 97
preterite 18, 19, 90–1
Prince Charles 160
printing 81

pronouns 3, 24, 25, 69–71, 95,
    102, 110–11
Proto-Germanic 15
Pullum, Geoffrey 165
punctuation 36, 124–30, 163–4
Pure English 9–11, 48, 50
Puttenham, George 82–3

Queen's English Society 49

Rae, Susan 88
reading programme 57–8
Received Pronunciation 76, 85–8,
    106, 132, 151
register 29, 35, 95, 98, 108, 119
rhoticity 106–7, 132, 135
runes 3, 26–7
Rushdie, Salman 144

Sanskrit 17
Scots 5–7, 101–4, 140
Scottish National Dictionary 103
Selfridges 158
Shakespeare, William 32, 56, 58–62,
    64, 70, 110, 133, 153
Shaw, George Bernard 13, 82, 84,
    151
Sheridan, Richard Brinsley 83
Sheridan, Thomas 84–5
Singlish 142–4, 145, 149
Skeat, W. W. 114
slang 42, 86, 136
social media 42, 121–4
Society for Pure English 48–9, 50
Spanish 32, 110, 133, 144, 149
spelling 1, 3, 5, 6, 8, 11, 17, 26–7,
    28, 30–3, 35–6, 80–2, 87, 89, 102,
    106–7, 120, 129–30, 134, 135,
    140, 151, 152–3

Spenser, Edmund 10, 56
split infinitives 50, 90, 91
Strunk, William Jr 54
superlatives 61, 64
Survey of English Dialects
    114–16
Sutherland, John 120
Swedish 17, 100
Swift, Jonathan 47–8, 49, 73

taboo 74, 108
Tebbit, Norman 159
tense 18–19, 61, 90–1, 95
Tesco 155
texting 11, 120, 123–4,
    126–7
Tok Pisin 7–8, 147–8
Tolkien, J. R. R. 92
Trevisa, John 105
Trudgill, Peter 106
Truss, Lynne 163–4
Turkish 32

Twitter 68, 121, 122,
    129–30

unique 64–5
Urban Dictionary 68–9

verbing 124–5

Waitrose 156, 158
Webster, Noah 93–4, 134
*Webster's Third New International
    Dictionary* 43–5
Welsh 20, 76
White, E. B. 54
Wiktionary 68–9
Wilson, Thomas 70
whom 96–8
World Standard English 151
Wright, Joseph 114, 116
Wyld, H. C. 73–4

Yiddish 133

Spenser, Edmund 30, 56
split infinitives 50, 90, 93
Strunk, William Jr. 54
superlatives 61, 94
Survey of English Dialects
  114–16
Sutherland, John 127
Swedish 12, 100
Swift, Jonathan 13, 36, 42

taboo ... 100
Taylor, Gordon 127
tense 10, 35, 81, 88, 118, 119
Tesco 122
texting 121, 122, 124–7
  126–7
Tok Pisin 7, 8, 14, 29
Tolkien, J. R. R. 92
Trevisa, John 105
Twaddell, Tony ...
Trim, Lynne 134–5
Turkish 12

Twitter 68, 121, 122,
  129–30

umlaut 64–5
Urban Dictionary 65–9

variation 114–5

Webster, Noah 136
Wedgwood 52, 55, 56, 57
Wemba ... (uncertain)
Welsh ...
Wells, J. C. 8
Whitman, Walt
Wilson, Thomas 29
yod ... 80–1
Word Standard English 127
Wright, Joseph 114, 116
Wyld, H. ... 114

Yiddish 100